INTRODUCTION TO
INTEGRATIVE
STUDIES

Marcus N. Tanner

Texas Tech University

Kendall Hunt
publishing company

Cover images © Shutterstock, Inc.

Kendall Hunt
publishing company

www.kendallhunt.com
Send all inquiries to:
4050 Westmark Drive
Dubuque, IA 52004-1840

I dedicate this book to the people who encourage me to be who I am without apology—my wife, Michelle, our two children, August and Aiden, and to my students.

I also want to acknowledge my parents who always told me I could do and be anything I wanted to be and who encouraged me to seek out information to find answers to my problems.

I also want to acknowledge my teaching assistants who have helped with different parts of this book project over the last several years—James, Grant, Kristina, Rachel, and Juliana.

CONTENTS

INTRODUCTION

Integrative Studies is a curricular approach to integrative learning and interdisciplinarity. To understand integrative studies, we must first understand its relation to interdisciplinarity. Frank (1988) in her article *Interdisciplinary: The first half-century* discusses the birth of the term *interdisciplinary*. It was likely first spoken at the Social Science Research Council (SSRC) in the mid-1920s. According to Frank, it was Professor Robert Sessions Woodworth that first used the term at a meeting of the SSRC in 1926. Woodward said,

> There is a certain limitation in the fact that we are in assembly of several disciplines . . . There would be no other body, unless we assume the function ourselves, charged with the duty of considering where the best chances were coordinated or interdisciplinary work. (Frank, 1988, p. 140)

The term interdisciplinary was likely first used, in written form, around 1937 (Augsburg, 2006). The concept of interdisciplinary existed prior to the SSRC conference, however. According to Frank (1988), George Ellery Hale, the first president of the National Research Council (NRC), discussed "subjects lying between the old-established divisions of science" in 1912. Between 1919 and 1929 new schools and institutes for social science research called for the integration of social sciences and related parts of industry, government, and public welfare. The most popular term in books published between 1925 and 1930 for interdisciplinary work was *cooperative research*. The first citation for interdisciplinary can be found in the December 1937 issue of the *Journal of Educational Sociology*. It was not until the mid-20th century that interdisciplinary became a common word in the social sciences. Frank (1988) noted interior designers were the most fervent interdisciplinarians of the 1970s. Although more discussion is provided concerning the definition of these important terms in the next chapter, it is important to briefly define the topic of this book. Interdisciplinarity is an approach to solving complex problems from multiple perspectives. Integration or integrative learning has a function within interdisciplinarity but is also extended to mean an application of interdisciplinarity. Interdisciplinarity and integrative learning can be applied to one's college curriculum. One way to do that is to choose a degree program that is specifically interdisciplinary. For example, many social science degree programs are interdisciplinary; human development and family studies, interior design, and hospitality. Degree programs that are in the sciences may also be interdisciplinary—neuropsychology and bioengineering, for example. There are also degree programs at many colleges and universities around the world that allow students to create their own program from courses that are offered on campus. These types of flexible degrees may be multidisciplinary or interdisciplinary. Some interdisciplinary programs have a unique focus on integrative learning.

There are many interdisciplinary (IDS) programs in the United States but not all IDS programs are structured the same or have the same benefits for students. Many of the IDS programs in higher education across the country might be considered by those who align themselves with the Association of Interdisciplinary Studies, as multidisciplinary programs rather than interdisciplinary. When students are searching for an interdisciplinary program, they should be aware of the differences between the terms interdisciplinary, multidisciplinary, cross-disciplinary, and transdisciplinary. These terms have meaning at different levels. For purposes of this introduction, their meaning is discussed at the program level.

Many multidisciplinary programs are structured in such a way that allows students to choose from many courses or specified series of courses (sometimes called concentrations or minors) in order to make up their degree. All students in this type of program usually take the required core courses but then create a degree program from several areas of concentration that makes sense for them and their interests or future career plans. Multidisciplinary students are largely left to themselves to create non-existent bridges across the different areas of course work. While multidisciplinary programs are attractive to many students, one major flaw is this lack of purposeful connection between the major coursework. For many programs across the country, neither is there much connection between the faculty teaching in a multidisciplinary program. Students in this type of program may have difficulty marketing themselves and their degree to potential employers because of a lack of a deliberate connection.

As one searches through the available interdisciplinary programs among colleges and universities in the United States, there seems to be two types of interdisciplinary programs. The first type is the program that looks much like the multidisciplinary program except a purposeful effort is made via the faculty or program staff to help students create a meaningful degree related to the student's career and future plans by choosing areas of study that can be easily connected to one another. This type of program seems more thoughtful than the multidisciplinary program discussed previously, however, it still has a flaw; there are no efforts made to teach students how to integrate their areas of concentration. There are some that would argue that without focused efforts toward integration, these efforts are also multidisciplinary at best. The second type of interdisciplinary program is much more purposeful than the first because the program is designed to allow students the flexibility to choose their areas of concentration but helps students learn the necessary skills needed to synthesize their course material. This type of program incorporates interdisciplinarity and integrative learning. The next section describes an Interdisciplinary Degree Program at Texas Tech University that requires students to take a series of Integrative Studies courses as an effort to help students create meaningful connections between their interdisciplinary coursework, co-curricular activities, and career and future plans.

University Studies at Texas Tech

What follows is a brief discussion of how the interdisciplinary program, known as University Studies, came into existence at Texas Tech. University Studies was created and approved as a degree program in early 2007. Since that time there have been a number of structural and organizational transitions to the program. When the degree was first created it could be better described as a multidisciplinary degree. Students were required to take core curriculum then choose three areas of concentration that comprised the 60-plus hours for a Bachelor of Arts or Science in University Studies (BUS). Other than an essay that students would write prior to admittance into the program, there were no faculty or staff working in the interest of students to help them synthesize their areas of concentration. In its humble beginnings, the program had less than 40 students, and in 2010 was transferred from the Provost Office to the University College, which at that time was a new experimental college on campus working to develop and provide a centralized structure for online programs.

After being transferred to the University College, there was a concerted and concentrated effort to help University Studies students create meaningful connections between their areas of study. Under the direction of the Associate Dean of the college, a director of advising was hired. At that time, newly admitted University Studies students were required to choose their areas of concentration in a way that seemed to make sense and write an essay describing how their choices were beneficial to their chosen career or future plans. The program began to grow and a number of advisors were hired to help students choose areas that made sense. Students and advisors worked together to create a meaningful degree plan. During this stage of the program's growth, it could be classified as the first type of interdisciplinary program discussed above. Other than advisors working with students to create meaningful degree programs, there were no efforts at integrating the knowledge of the chosen areas of study. There were no attempts made to connect students' learning to their career and future plans. Because all of the courses were offered online by different programs across the university, faculty would not know that a student was a University Studies student. The result was students were taking online courses from across the campus and had no skills to integrate the knowledge they were receiving across the curriculum. The new college experienced turnover in the Dean's office within a year of its creation. In 2011, a new interim dean and associate dean were hired. In June of that year, University College hired its first program director for Integrative Studies. Integrative Studies was little more than a way for University College to develop online courses that would meet the needs of students who needed to graduate. The original idea behind Integrative Studies was to create online writing-intensive courses that were not available to students to take in other departments. New course development was spurred by the student need for degree completion.

Very quickly, it was recognized that students needed more than writing-intensive courses. They needed a way to synthesize their chosen areas of study in a way that made sense to their career and future plans. From that need came the creation of a series of courses that would be required as the core curriculum of the University Studies degree. These integrative studies courses would help students synthesize their areas of study. Students would take their 60 hours of core curriculum, 12 hours of Integrative Studies, and 18 hours from each of three areas of study. The three areas of study must have some logical fit and have some application for future study or a career. It was important to help students create a meaningful, customizable, interdisciplinary degree that would have implications for their career and future plans. It was the development of the Integrative Studies program that would help elevate the BUS degree towards the second type of IDS program. This new BUS degree program is more than a degree completion program; it is purposeful, where students learn skills they need to synthesize learning across their areas of study. More than that, students engage in integrative learning that helps them apply their knowledge and skills outside the classroom. They have the opportunity to be engaged in undergraduate research, service learning, internships, and independent learning projects.

Integrative Studies at Texas Tech

The Integrative Studies (INTS) program is an official minor that any student on the TTU campus may choose as part of their degree, however it is designed specifically for interdisciplinary students. For students who were admitted to the program beginning in the Fall of 2012, they are required to take the core courses for the BUS program, and 12 hours of INTS; *2310—Foundations of Integrative Studies, 3300—Perspective on Integrative Studies*, choose from *3301—Career and Professional Development* or *4320—Internship*, and *4350—Capstone in Integrative Studies*. The program also offers three additional courses; *3330—Global Perspectives, 3350 - Team Leadership*, and *4000—Independent Studies*. The Global Perspectives course is also offered with a service learning component.

Interdisciplinarity is an approach to answering questions, solving problems, and addressing contemporary social issues from multiple perspectives. Interdisciplinarians combine two or more academic disciplines or fields of study, professions, technologies, departments, or the like in an effort to solve these complex problems or provide new insights of understanding. Students in the Integrative Studies program are challenged to bring together or incorporate their disciplinary insights into a new holistic framework for understanding complex problems. The Integrative Studies program helps students develop the intellectual tools needed to build bridges across academic disciplines and apply their skills, innovations, and knowledge in various academic and practical settings. In core classes, students develop portfolio artifacts that showcase each individual's skills, interests, and talents. The portfolio and applied learning experiences provide each student with valuable resources for flexible, individualized career planning and development. A brief description of each INTS course is offered below.

INTS 2310 introduces students to the foundations of integrative studies. In this course, students learn the developmental process of integrative studies, the fundamentals of interdisciplinary research, and the integration of personal, educational, and professional goals. This course is designed to provide students with the essential principles and concepts of integrative studies that will serve as the foundation for their future careers in the professional field of their choice.

INTS 3300 provides students with an intermediate experience in the interdisciplinary research process. In this course students learn to develop important and complex research questions that can be answered using an interdisciplinary approach to research. Students taking this course are expected to develop an interdisciplinary research proposal.

INTS 3301 provides students the necessary career management skills for workplace success. This course helps students evaluate their future career and professional plans. Students learn how to develop career and professional goals, research career and professional opportunities, and develop and compile artifacts that will be necessary for interviewing for a career or educational placement. They also identify and describe important steps to making a career or professional transition. This course is designed to be useful to students taking it as an elective or those taking it as part of the series of Integrative Studies courses. Students concentrating a portion of their degree program in Integrative Studies should take this course before signing up for INTS 4320: Internship in Integrative Studies.

INTS 3330 presents global issues and the importance of being multi-culturally competent. It emphasizes interdisciplinary problem-solving through critical, analytical, and integrative approaches to the study of general issues and trends facing the contemporary world. Students will explore significant issues that are shaped by global forces and international institutions and how the United States is impacted by and connected to those issues.

INTS 3350 presents a model for interdisciplinary leadership. This course will emphasize the practices of highly effective and exemplary leadership through interdisciplinary teams. Students will utilize critical, analytical, and integrative approaches to interdisciplinary problem solving.

INTS 4320 allows students to apply program course material and integrative studies to researching a workplace problem, while at the same time gaining valuable work experience. The advantage to doing an internship with a research component is that it allows the student to apply and showcase interdisciplinary skills to a potential employer. Students in this course will be expected to identify an interdisciplinary problem in their workplace. Students in this course will be expected to spend a portion of their internship researching the problem and presenting potential solutions to their employer at the end of the internship.

INTS 4350 provides students the opportunity to weave together their academic/professional career to create one cohesive narrative. It is in this course that students will have the opportunity to interlace common threads that showcase their education, skills, and abilities. Students will be expected to develop an integrated omnibus portfolio of their educational and professional career. Students will also be expected to showcase their interdisciplinary experience via a video presentation.

Since the Fall of 2011 the faculty and staff of University Studies has continued to develop the INTS curriculum and enroll record numbers of students. As Integrative Learning is a growing field of scholarship that prepares students for the challenges and complexity of the 21st century, INTS courses were developed using the Association of American Colleges and Universities (AAC&U) Liberal Education and America's Promise (LEAP) initiative.

AAC&U and LEAP

"Liberal Education and America's Promise (LEAP) is a national advocacy, campus action, and research initiative that champions the importance of a twenty-first century liberal education—for individuals and for a nation dependent on economic creativity and democratic vitality" (AAC&U 2005). The economy is changing in the United States; as a result, the characteristics of the workforce needed is also being modified. Employers are demanding different skills and knowledge from their college-educated workforce. College graduates will be expected to know more about more. They will be expected to have strong intellectual, transferable, and serviceable skills to maneuver challenging and global environments successfully.

The AAC&U through LEAP is helping to transform traditional education in the United States. LEAP helps students achieve a set of Essential Learning Outcomes no matter what their chosen field of study is. This is important to students in an IDS program such as University Studies, as they do not have a typical field of study. Rather, students craft their own degree in such a way that incorporates multiple fields of study. The challenge for many IDS programs across the country is to provide flexible degree programs that allow students to create their own degree while maintaining an overall sense of purpose for the degree, rigorous study, and connections between chosen areas of study. The LEAP Essential Learning Outcomes (ELOs) may help curriculum developers do just that. Furthermore, students may utilize these learning outcomes as a way to take ownership and responsibility over their education.

For example, curriculum developers might utilize the Integrative Learning VALUE Rubric to measure student success in an interdisciplinary program with a focus on integrative learning. AAC&U defines Integrative Learning as "an understanding and a disposition that a student builds across the curriculum and co-curriculum, from making simple connections among ideas and experiences to synthesizing and transferring learning to new, complex situations within and beyond the campus." Interdisciplinary students should be able to meet the benchmark of the Integrative Learning Rubric; be able to identify connections between life and school; present information from more than one field of study or perspective; transfer skills, abilities, theories or methodologies from one situation to another; use integrated communication in assignments; and describe performance through reflection and self-assessment.

As interdisciplinary programs focus more on integrative learning, students may be helped to understand more about their interdisciplinary degree and how it may be useful to their future. Integrative learning programs help students construct a partnership between their education and their career and future plans. Specifically, the University Studies program at Texas Tech focuses on several of the expected learning outcomes (ELOs) with plans to incorporate more as the program grows. As expected, we highlight Integrative and Applied Learning. Our overall goal is to help students demonstrate an "application of knowledge, skills, and responsibilities to new settings and complex problems" across their general and specialized course work.

Integrative learning programs may also help students prepare for new challenges by teaching them intellectual and practical skills including: inquiry and analysis, critical and creative thinking, written and oral communication, teamwork, and problem solving. Interdisciplinary programs like the one at George Mason University help students engage in personal and social responsibility by engaging them in ethical reasoning, intercultural awareness, service learning, and study abroad. Integrative learning programs should challenge students to become lifelong learners and to become actively involved in diverse communities around the world. These types of skills will help students achieve personal success, as they define it, and by engaging in complex problem solving our world may become a better place for all.

The Interdisciplinary/Integrative Learning program curriculum provides students a common body of knowledge for recognizing various disciplinary perspectives as well as learning how to synthesize and evaluate those perspectives, thus empowering students to address meaningful and complex issues in new and unique ways. Students completing this type program are believed to be better educated for addressing the increasingly complex and interdisciplinary challenges of the ever-expanding and interwoven world economy and will have enhanced marketability for a wide range of careers. Some students may also be better prepared to enter graduate programs related to their areas of study.

Because of the purposive flexibility of interdisciplinary/integrative learning degrees like University Studies, many graduates leave their university prepared for their next steps in life, whether employment in an entry-level position, opportunities for promotion and career advancement, or for graduate studies in a variety of disciplines. As the marketplace becomes more and more diverse, employers are increasingly looking for individuals who are comfortable working across a wide array of disciplines and can smoothly transition from one thing to the next. Interdisciplinarity and integrative learning has become more important in the undergraduate curriculum because the need for broad-based skills and knowledge is pervasive. In *Contemporary Understandings of General Education* (1998), Carol Schneider and Robert Schoenberg write about the need for the capacity to cross boundaries, explore connections, and move in uncharted directions. American higher education is in a period of transformative change. Integration of learning is central to this change. Integrative learning creates awareness of relationships, tensions, and complementarities among ideas. It generates links among previously unconnected issues, approaches, sources of knowledge, and contexts of practice.

Integrative learning curriculum helps prepare students for current and future job demand as well as long-term careers. Graduates should have acquired important skills that employers value. Diplomaguide.com notes that the ability to learn quickly, see connections among concepts, and adapt to changing situations involves skills that are applicable to many careers ("Bachelor of Interdisciplinary Studies," 2011). According to PayScale.com, in a survey named PayScale College Salary Report, Interdisciplinary studies was rated one of the top best undergrad college degrees by salary ("PayScale college Salary Report," 2012).

Conclusion

Now that you understand a little more about different types of multidisciplinary and interdisciplinary programs, how they can be useful, and general expectations for you as a student, we will move on to the subject matter of this textbook. The textbook is separated into four parts.

Part I, which includes Chapters 1–5, is an introduction to interdisciplinary and integrative learning. Chapter 1 focuses on helping students define the concepts of interdisciplinarity, integration, and integrative learning. In addition, this chapter defines related concepts and terms that are important for students of integrative studies. In Chapter 2, students will learn about the history of interdisciplinarity. The chapter is framed against the backdrop of historical figures like Leonardo daVinci and Plato. Discussed in this chapter is the trajectory of academia, the creation of disciplines, and the subsequent development of interdisciplinarity and integrative learning. In Chapter 3, students will be introduced to several theories that may provide a framework for interdisciplinary and integrative studies. Example theories presented in this chapter are Complex Systems Theory and Ecological Systems Theory. In Chapter 4, students are introduced to the concepts of epistemology and critical thinking. The concepts are defined and then used to provide students with additional insights relevant to integrative learning. In Chapter 5, students will explore integrative learning and its application to academics, life, and work experiences. Although each chapter does so, this particular chapter highlights student successes as integrative learning.

Part II of this textbook, comprised of Chapters 6–8 provides an overview of interdisciplinary research. In Chapter 6, students are acclimated to basic research methods common to all types of research. In Chapter 7, students are introduced to several models of interdisciplinary research, including Repko's (2012) 10 step Interdisciplinary Research Process. I have endeavored to simplify the process for purposes of this introductory text. Chapter 8 finalizes Part II by discussing concepts related to interdisciplinary research; knowledge transfer, conditions for integration, finding common ground between disciplinary insights, and providing new integrative insights to complex problem solving.

Part III is comprised of Chapters 9–11 where the focus is to discuss interdisciplinary priorities. Interdisciplinary priorities are skills and abilities that are characteristic and critical for interdisciplinarians to possess. Chapter 9 focuses on the advantages and disadvantages of interdisciplinarity and integrative studies. The chapter presents both sides of the argument but helps students make the case for interdisciplinarity. This chapter is helpful to students who struggle with the purpose of interdisciplinarity and framing their learning experiences as integrative learners. The chapter will also highlight characteristics that comprise typical interdisciplinary and integrative learners. For example, they have a love of learning. This particular characteristic leads students to be lifelong learners. In the global environment in which we live, having a broader perspective on complex problems should be a priority for integrative learners. Thus, in Chapter 10, students are presented with the need for a global perspective in problem solving. In addition, students will explore the nature of interdisciplinary teams and the characteristics that integrative learners typically possess in order to lead such teams. Chapter 11 bridges Part III and Part IV by helping students reflect on the discontinuous nature of their own academic, work, and life experiences. Additionally, students will utilize previous learning from this textbook to develop continuity from their discontinuous experiences. Not only does this chapter help students construct a story of who they are as an integrative learner but it provides a framework for Part IV where they will develop materials directly related to life after graduation.

Finally, **Part IV** helps students develop themselves as interdisciplinarians. Chapters 12–15 will help students learn to connect different areas of their life, tell their interdisciplinary story, and construct a meaningful portfolio. Chapter 12 provides further argument for the value of interdisciplinary and integrative learning. Chapters 13 and 14 help students develop materials for next steps after graduation. These chapters are particularly focused on helping students develop a resume and cover letter that are focused but takes into account the interdisciplinary nature of their experiences. Also discussed is the importance of portfolio development, especially for interdisciplinary and integrative learners. A process for collecting and developing artifacts is included in the chapter. Chapter 15 provides helpful information about graduate school and typical processes for applying and being accepted into programs. The chapter helps students focus their next steps and utilize their interdisciplinarity and integrative learning skills to improve opportunities.

References

Augsburg, T. (2006). *Becoming interdisciplinary: An introduction to interdisciplinary studies* (2nd ed.). Dubuque, IA: Kendall Hunt.

Bachelor of Interdisciplinary Studies. (2011). Retrieved from http://diplomaguide.com

Frank, R. (1988). Interdisciplinary: The first half century. *Issues in Integrative Studies, 6,* 91–101.

PayScale college Salary Report. (2012). Retrieved from http://www.payscale.com/best-colleges/degrees.asp

Schneider, C. G., & Shoenberg, R. (1998). Contemporary Understandings of Liberal Education: The Academy in Transition.

PART I

Interdisciplinarity & Integrative Learning

CHAPTER 1

Defining Integrative and Interdisciplinary Studies

The terms *integrative* and *interdisciplinary studies* refer to a particular approach of study. Repko, Szostak, and Buchberger (2013) define interdisciplinary studies as "a particular approach to study that is distinct from disciplinary approaches" (p. 24). They go on to describe it as an approach that integrates disciplinary insights as a process approach to studying complex problems. One of the reasons interdisciplinarity is so useful is because of the wealth of complex problems faced by humanity. Complex problems exist at every level of life; individually, systematically, as in our family, workplace, schools, and at larger levels like government and society. What does it mean to be an interdisciplinarian? Interdisciplinarians are those who recognize the need for and utilize multiple perspectives to solve complex problems. As interdisciplinarians, we think of some problems as complex because they cannot be solved or adequately understood by using one perspective.

Integrative learning according to Veronica Boix-Mansilla (2010), is "when [students] can bring together concepts, methods, or languages from two or more disciplines or established areas of expertise in order to explain a phenomenon, solve a problem, create a product, or raise a new question" (p. 13). What does it mean to be an integrative learner? An integrative learner is one who is able to absorb and apply multiple knowledges across multiple experiences in order to solve complex problems. In other words, integrative learners are able to use disciplinary insights and perspectives to create new holistic frameworks for studying and solving complex problems and issues.

At your work, you may also come across a complex problem that does not make sense to solve using one perspective. Using an interdisciplinary approach can be very beneficial, very helpful to you and to your workplace. Interdisciplinarians are constantly challenged to create something new and unique from multiple perspectives. To do this well you must be able to see the connections that others do not. Newell (1999) describes interdisciplinary study as providing one form of integrative learning limited to drawing from academic disciplines.

It can be confusing to discuss both interdisciplinarity and integration in the same textbook or course. In the relevant literature, the terms *interdisciplinary* and *integration* are sometimes

FIGURE 1.1   A Continuum of Study

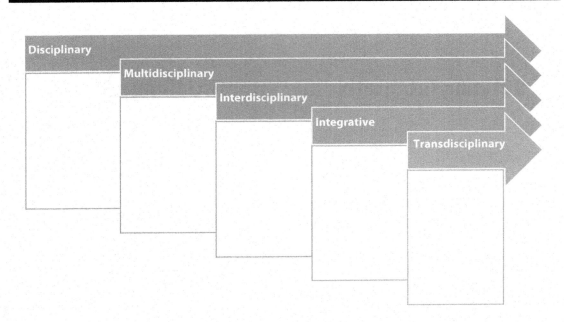

used interchangeably, but they are different, and they mean different things. Here is one way to view the two terms. Academically speaking, interdisciplinary students typically have more than one area of study as part of their degree program. Each area of study works together to form one degree. It is the synthesizing or the bringing together of those areas of study that is integration. Integration is part of an interdisciplinary process that leads to the solution or a new understanding of a complex problem. However, integrative learning goes beyond the interdisciplinary process and requires the use of multiple knowledges and multiple experiences as an application of interdisciplinarity to complex problems.

In this chapter, you will learn to define the terms and concepts related to interdisciplinarity and integrative learning. Figure 1.1 provides one way to view the different terms and concepts we will learn about in this chapter. Use the empty boxes to write in key terms related to each of the concepts.

One way to define integrative studies is that it provides for a synthesis of study and life, an application of interdisciplinarity to complex problems. Integrative studies provides for a common body of knowledge recognizing various disciplinary perspectives, as well as learning how to synthesize and evaluate those perspectives. Thus, empowering people to address meaningful and complex issues in new and unique ways. As you continue to progress through your educational program, consider how your disciplinary concentrations intersect, and how you can synthesize or weave together your educational, personal, and professional experiences. Augsburg (2006) provided the following model of interdisciplinarity (see Figure 1.2).

FIGURE 1.2

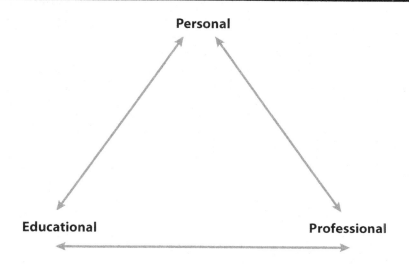

Personal

Educational

Professional

FIGURE 1.3 Integrative Learning

Feng Yu/Shutterstock, Inc.

Perhaps Figure 1.3 more accurately represents integration, being able to weave together your education and life experiences as a weaver integrates multiple threads to create new products. Integrative learners are able to utilize an intellectual process of weaving to create personal narratives for use in discussing career and future plans from an interdisciplinary perspective. So integrative learning connects or weaves together your classroom and out-of-classroom experiences. Consider the parallels that you might draw from your experiences and what you are learning in the classroom that can help you provide insight into complex problems.

At first, it may seem like interdisciplinarians as students are at a disadvantage. How will you explain your degree program to a potential employer? How will you connect your areas of study in a way that make sense for your future plans? The truth is, we all have disconnected experiences both in school and in life. One skill that integrative learners have is to be able to take seemingly disconnected experiences and weave them together into a cohesive narrative that makes sense for career and future plans. Integrative learners are able to ask meaningful questions about complex issues and problems. Integrative learners have the ability to locate multiple sources of knowledge, information, and perspectives and create new and unique ways of looking at problems.

Interdisciplinarians and integrative learners are valuable to our society. An interdisciplinary degree can be very valuable to you and some employers. We will discuss the disadvantages and advantages of interdisciplinarity in a later chapter. However, as our world becomes increasingly interconnected, social problems become bigger and more complex. As problems become more complex they will require insights from multiple disciplines or multiple perspectives in order to solve or better understand them. Even if you were to look at problems in your local workplace, these problems too are becoming more multifaceted where they cannot be solved using one perspective. Interdisciplinarians then are at an advantage. Employers are valuing the ability of employees who are flexible and are able to see problems and issues from multiple perspectives and who can connect that information in order to solve problems in the workplace. Employers are looking for workers with intercultural awareness and cultural sensitivity; those who have knowledge about diverse peoples and practices. While interdisciplinarians and integrative learners may not be experts in any one field they are able to locate and apply multiple knowledges in useful ways. As we continue to move through this chapter, we will define important terms and concepts useful to interdisciplinarians and integrative learners. It is important to begin with the definition of a discipline.

Disciplinarity

Understanding interdisciplinarity is dependent on an understanding of the "nature of academic disciplines and their influence on faculty life in colleges and universities" (Lattuca, 2001, p. 278). A **discipline** is a field of study; it provides the conceptual structure for learning, an instructive community and a communication network. A discipline can be defined as a system of knowledge specialties. There are categories of disciplines; Natural Sciences, Social Sciences, and Humanities, for example. Each of these categories includes a system of knowledge unique to its conceptual structure. Social science includes disciplines such as Anthropology, Economics, Communication Studies, Psychology, and Sociology. Disciplines are also a cultural system that is created over time as disciplinary knowledge is organized and transmitted to its students. Disciplines are "social groupings of people who, to varying extents, share assumptions, behavior patterns, and beliefs about scholarship" (Lattuca, 2001, loc 409). In the late 17th and 18th centuries, the Enlightenment aided the growth of disciplines both within and outside of science. The notion that people could find answers to complex problems by means of their reason fostered the view that limiting scholars' fields of inquiry and systematizing knowledge into categories was indispensable to progress. In modern day universities, departments became the channels through which academic resources flowed, and they, combined with new journals, some of them published by departments and some by disciplinary societies, became the arbiters of academic quality. So today we see universities organized by colleges. Colleges are then organized by departments using a conceptual structure.

Interdisciplinary study focuses on disciplinary insights and knowledge that is not easily uncovered. Interdisciplinarians and integrative learners are forced to consider the assumptions and conventions that comprise the disciplines; their problems, methods, research practices, bodies of knowledge, or even social networks (Lattuca, 2001, loc 278).

Crossdisciplinarity

Crossdisciplinary is another important term in understanding integrative and interdisciplinary studies. It has been used for several different purposes:

> to view one discipline from the perspective of another, rigid axiomatic control by one discipline, the solution of a problem with no intention of generating a new science or paradigm, new fields that develop between two or more disciplines, a generic adjective for six different categories of discipline-crossing activities, and a generic adjective for all activities involving interaction across disciplines. (Klein, 1990, p. 55)

Lattuca (2001, loc 944) discussed crossdisciplinarity as informed disciplinarity in teaching and research. In teaching, faculty would utilize examples from other disciplines in ways that did not change the focus of the class from one discipline to another. In research, questions might be informed by concepts and theories from other disciplines. Research methods from other disciplines might also be used. "Mere borrowing of methods, theories, concepts, or other disciplinary components to conduct research or teach a course is not sufficient for interdisciplinarity" (loc 952).

Multidisciplinary

Multidisciplinary is the utilization of multiple disciplines to study a problem without an effort towards integration or synthesis. It is a juxtaposition of disciplines. It is additive, not integrative. The disciplinary knowledge is considered to be mutual and cumulative, not interactive. "In multidisciplinary or thematic approaches to learning, students examine a topic through distinct disciplinary perspectives but do not seek to make connections across such perspectives" (Boix-Mansilla, 2010, p. 16).

Interdisciplinarity

Klein and Newell (1997) define interdisciplinary studies as

> a process of answering a question, solving a problem, or addressing a topic that is too broad or complex to be dealt with adequately by a single discipline or profession . . . [it] draws on disciplinary perspectives and integrates their insights through the construction of a more comprehensive perspective. (pp. 393–394)

Repko (2012) defines it as

> a process of answering a question, solving a problem, or addressing a topic that is too broad or complex to be dealt with adequately by a single discipline, and draws on the disciplines with the goal of integrating their insights to construct a more comprehensive understanding. (p. 16)

The aim of interdisciplinary studies is to construct a more comprehensive perspective or understanding. Augsburg (2006) characterizes interdisciplinary as providing for a method of solving a complex problem that draws on several disciplinary perspectives, disciplines, or systems of knowledge. Interdisciplinarity works toward the integration of these disciplinary perspectives. Disciplinary perspectives are synthesized in order to solve complex problems. As a result, connecting or complimenting and supplementing the limits of individual disciplinary approaches to solving complex problems.

The Oxford English dictionary defines interdisciplinary as, "relating to more than one branch of knowledge" ("interdisciplinary," April 2010). Dictionary definitions tend to be too ambiguous regarding what is being combined within disciplines or how the combination is accomplished. Other definitions specify integration of different disciplines as the litmus test for interdisciplinarity. Lattuca (2001) defined interdisciplinarity as the interaction of different disciplines (loc 911). Even as we study interdisciplinarity, we will learn that scholars disagree on the definition and application of interdisciplinarity.

Rhoten, Boix Mansilla, Chun, and Klein (2006) define interdisciplinary studies as

> a mode of curriculum design and instruction in which individual faculty or teams identify, evaluate, and integrate information, data, techniques, tools, perspectives, concepts, or theories from two or more disciplines or bodies of knowledge to advance students' capacity to understand issues, address problems, and create new approaches and solutions that extend beyond the scope of a single discipline or area of instruction. (p. 3)

Repko et. al. (2014) present an integrated definition of interdisciplinary studies, "a cognitive process by which individuals or groups draw on disciplinary perspectives and integrate their insights and modes of thinking to advance their understanding of a complex problem with the goal of applying the understanding to a real-world problem" (p 28).

There are two forms of interdisciplinarity: instrumental interdisciplinarity and conceptual interdisciplinarity. Instrumental interdisciplinarity might be defined as a pragmatic approach that focuses on interdisciplinary problem solving activity and does not seek synthesis or fusion of different perspectives (Salter & Hearn, 1997). Conceptual interdisciplinarity emphasizes the synthesis of knowledge, a "theoretical, primarily epistemological enterprise involving internal coherence, the development of new conceptual categories, methodological unification, and long term research and exploration" (Salter & Hearn, 1997, p. 9).

Integrative Studies

Well-equipped students are integrative thinkers who can see connections in contrasting information and by drawing on multiple sources of information, knowledge, and perspectives to make decisions and solve problems. This requires them to be intentional about the process of learning, empowered by the mastery of intellectual and practical skills, informed by knowledge from various disciplines, and responsible for their actions and those of society. Schneider (2004) defined integrative learning as a

> shorthand term for teaching a set of capacities—capacities we might also call the arts of connection, reflective judgment, and considered action—that enables graduates to put their knowledge to effective use . . . it should also lead students to connect and integrate the different parts of their overall education, to connect learning with the world beyond the academy, and above all, to translate their education to new contexts, new problems, new responsibilities. (pp 1–2)

It can be confusing discussing both interdisciplinarity and integration. They are often used interchangeably in the literature. Klein (2005) discusses integrative studies as the broader of the two terms; as an umbrella term for structures, strategies, and activities that bridge numerous divides: high school and college, general education and majors, and experiences in and out of the classroom.

Integrative Studies has been defined as providing for a synthesis of study and life, an application of interdisciplinarity to complex problems. Furthermore, Integrative Studies provides for a common body of knowledge, recognizing various disciplinary perspectives as well as learning how to synthesize and evaluate those perspectives, thus empowering people to address meaningful and complex issues in new and unique ways (Hughes, Munoz, & Tanner, 2015). Integrative Studies as a field can be found as part of university programs designed to help you uncover and weave together the common threads of your life—educationally, professionally, and experientially.

Transdisciplinary

Transdisciplinarity is highly contested and is employed differently by scholars. This concept is different from interdisciplinarity in that it produces new knowledge by applying interdisciplinary integration methods to societal problems. Transdisciplinary studies utilize conceptual frameworks that transcend the narrow scope of disciplinary world views, encompassing the several parts of material handled separately by specialized disciplines. Bergmann et al. (2012) describe transdisciplinary research as a "new mode of the production of knowledge" (p. 14). Tress, Tress, and Fry (2007) define transdisciplinarity as

> Involving academic researchers from different unrelated disciplines as well as nonacademic participants, such as land managers, user groups, and the general public, to create new knowledge and theory and delve into a common question. Transdisciplinarity thus combines interdisciplinarity with a participatory approach. (p. 374)

Lattuca (2001) described transdisciplinary research as being "driven by a belief that natural and social systems, such as those studied in economics, biology, and physics, have common underlying structures or relationships" (loc 1070). Thus a concept, theory, or method could be applied across disciplines. Miller (1982) applied transdisciplinary to structuralism, general systems, and sociobiology in a comprehensive effort to identify connections and underlying similarities in natural and social phenomena (in Lattuca, 2001).

Conclusion

Now that you understand a little more about the terminology related to integrative and interdisciplinary studies, we will discuss in the next chapter the history of interdisciplinarity and integrative learning. It is important to understand that interdisciplinary and integrative studies are not necessarily new fields of study. They have been in existence since people began collecting and publishing their knowledge.

References

Augsburg, T. (2006). *Becoming interdisciplinary: An introduction to interdisciplinary studies* (2nd ed.). Dubuque, IA: Kendall Hunt.

Bergmann, M., Jahn, T., Knobloch, T., Krohn, W., Pohl, C., & Schramm, E. (2012). *Methods for transdiciplinary research: A primer for practice* (R.C. Faust, Trans.). Frankfurt, Germany: Campus Verlag.

Boix-Mansilla, V. (2010). MYP guide to interdisciplinary teaching and learning. Cardiff, Wales.

Hughes, P. C., Munoz, J. M., & Tanner, M. N. (Eds.). (2015). *Perspectives in Interdisciplinary and Integrative Studies*. Lubbock, TX: Texas Tech University Press.

Interdisciplinary. (2013). In *Oxford English Dictionary* (7th ed.). Oxford, UK: Oxford University Press.

Klein, J. T. (2005). Integrative learning and interdisciplinary studies. *Peer Review, 7*(4), 8–10.

Klein, J. T., & Newell, W. H. (1997). Advancing interdisciplinary studies. In Jerry G. Gaff & James L. Ratcliff (Eds.), *Handbook of the Undergraduate Curriculum: A Comprehensive Guide to the Purposes, Structures, Practices, and Change* (pp. 393–415). San Francisco, CA: Jossey-Bass.

Lattuca, L. R. (2001). *Creating interdisciplinarity: Interdisciplinary research and teaching among college and university faculty.* Nashville, TN: Vanderbilt University Press.

Miller, R. C. (1982). Varieties of interdisciplinary approaches in the social sciences: a 1981 overview. *Issues in Integrative Studies, 1*, 1–37.

Newell, W. H. (1999). The Promise of Integrative Learning. *About campus, 4*(2), 17–23.

Repko, A. F. (2012). *Interdisciplinary research: Process and theory* (2nd ed.). Thousand Oaks, CA: Sage Publications, Inc.

Repko, A. F., Szostak, R. R., & Buchberger, M. P. (2013). *Introduction to interdisciplinary studies.* Thousand Oaks, CA: Sage publications, Inc.

Rhoten, D., Boix Mansilla, V., Chun, M., & Klein, J. T. (2006). Interdisciplinary education at liberal arts institutions. *Teagle Foundation White Paper.* Retrieved June, 13, 2007.

Salter, L., & Hearn, A. (1997). *Outside the lines: Issues in interdisciplinary research*: McGill-Queen's Press-MQUP.

Schneider, C. G. (2004). Practicing liberal education: Formative themes in the re-invention of liberal learning. *Liberal Education, 90(2).*

Tress, G., Tress, B., & Fry, G. (2007). Analysis of the barriers to integration in landscape research projects. *Land use policy, 24*(2), 374–385.

CHAPTER 2

History of Interdisciplinarity

Julie Thompson Klein in her book *Interdisciplinarity*, quotes Georges Gusdorf in her chapter on The Evolution of Interdisciplinarity: "the need for interdisciplinarity has been reflected in the epistemological writings ever since the origins of Western science" (Klein, 1990, p. 19). Klein admits that understanding the concept of interdisciplinarity is complicated because of its unknown origin. Some have found interdisciplinarity originating in the philosophical ideas of Plato, Aristotle, Kant, and Hegel. Others view interdisciplinarity as a notion of the 20th century liberal education. Klein's view is that the concept of interdisciplinarity was already contained in the major ideas of Greek philosophy. It is not that they used the word interdisciplinarity, but the idea or concept of interdisciplinarity was already contained in those early philosophies. Klein bridges a gap between the ideas of interdisciplinarity being old, yet understanding the, "problem of knowledge that informs the modern concept of interdisciplinarity." Gunn (1992) does not view interdisciplinary studies, in the strict sense, as a field. He viewed origins of interdisciplinarity "more in terms of boundary crossing and borrowing, particularly in the area of humanities" (Augsburg, 2006, p. 5). Other scholars, Augsburg and Newell, for example, find Klein and Gunn's concepts of interdisciplinarity to be problematic as they are antiquated. Specifically, Newell (1998) discusses the fact that interdisciplinarity could not have existed before there were disciplines. Yet, interdisciplinarity implies the use of multiple perspectives or knowledges not just multiple disciplines to solve complex problems. Throughout the history of education one can find the notion of interdisciplinarity emerging from unified and fragmented knowledges.

Early Civilization Education

The earliest civilizations began in the Middle East about 3000 BCE. Exploring the history of some of the earliest civilizations, we know that education was indispensable to monumental development of their society. In Egyptian culture, education was preserved and controlled primarily by priests. Priests taught in formal schools such practical subjects like science, medicine, mathematics, and geometry. In Egypt there were only two types of formal schooling one for scribes and one for training future priests. Education in Mesopotamia was very similar to that of Egypt in that education was aimed at training scribes and priests. Even as we learn about new civilizations such as the Mayans, Aztecs, and Incas, we know that they too relied heavily on training scribes and priests who would provide education for privileged youth. Although we can see that training or education was in a number of subjects, divisions of knowledge did not exist during this time. All who would be educated learned all of the existing knowledge. Further, what we can extract or deduce from this information is that educated people at this time could be called interdisciplinarians as they utilized multiple knowledges or perspectives to operate in their environment.

Ancient Hebrew culture also relied upon religious priests as the educators of their time. Priests trained scribes who became the representatives of education. They were specialized and professional; writing letters and contracts for those who acquired their services. They maintained records and prepared orders as servants of the king. They copied sacred law and established canonical texts. Scribes were also the ones who translated the Hebrew Bible into Greek.

Greek Education

Greek society brought about the master to pupil or apprentice type of education. Young men were educated through the counsel of older men. By studying 4th century education practices, one can see where knowledge was separated into subjects. Young Athenians were apprentices but they would be taken to different masters. For example, they learned the elements of literacy from the *grammatistes*. They would learn more advanced forms of literacy from poets or historians. They were also instructed in physical and military activities.

Higher education, for those who could afford it, emerged with the appearance of the Sophists who were professional educators. They argued for an education that was more practical in nature. During that time, practicality meant learning to be a successful politician.

It was at the beginning of the 4th century that education became organized along definitive lines. Plato, a student of Socrates opened his school, the Academy around 387 (Cherniss, 1944). Plato was perhaps the first to advocate philosophy as a unifying science. The philosopher is one who is capable of synthesizing knowledge and believed that only those who can attain an understanding of genuine reality through the study of dialectics and mathematical reasoning were fit for the highest offices of the state (Cross, 1964). The idea of synthesizing knowledge can be seen in the practice of most doctoral programs today.

Aristotle, Plato's student, believed that it was important to define clear divisions of inquiry. He was less concerned with the search for ideas and more so with logical structure, classification, and systemization. So he divided knowledge into three categories, in descending order of status: theoretical (including theology, mathematics, and physics), practical (including ethics and politics), and productive (including fine arts, poetics, and engineering), with philosophy considered the branch of knowledge that would bring all other knowledge together. This idea of philosophy as an integrative field persisted until the 19th century.

Medieval Education

Charlemagne in power during the 8th century was a great proponent of education. It was under his rule that clergy be educated in Latin and the correct use of language. Here is where we also see the rise of the priests or clergy as educators of society once again. It was generally accepted that the church had the authority in matters of belief, conduct, and education.

Renaissance

During the renaissance of the 12th century, education was offered to members of the clergy. Some chose to exist within monastic culture. Others who were interested in social advancement or material profits entered newly established schools for notaries and law. These schools were organized under the protection of the church. There were schools for secular subjects directed by an archdeacon. These urban schools were highly successful and necessitated the licensing of teaching; which were conferred by the bishop of the church. The more gifted clerics were able to extend their studies in the liberal arts. At that time, the trivium was comprised of grammar, rhetoric, and logic. The quadrivium included geometry, arithmetic, harmonics, and astronomy. Once students completed their liberal arts training, they studied philosophy. Philosophy was comprised of the Aristotlian division with a fourth being labeled mechanical, which included processing wood, navigation, agriculture, and medicine.

Although there are a number of important historical figures of the renaissance, one of particular note is Leonardo da Vinci. da Vinci was a painter, sculptor, architect, musician, mathematician, engineer, inventor, anatomists, geologist, cartographer, botanists, and writer. He has been considered to be one of the greatest polymaths of all time. Polymathy in Greek means having learned much. It is a person whose knowledge extends across many different subject areas. A polymath is also a person known to draw on complex bodies of knowledge to solve specific problems, an interdisciplinarian. He is a renowned painter, having very famous paintings all over the world, most notably the Mona Lisa and The Last Supper. He is also revered for his technological ingenuity; many of his inventions have gone on to be recreated from his original ideas. He could be thought as one of the very early interdisciplinarians of our world.

Reformation

It was during the reformation that new political and social systems broke away from the Roman Catholic Church. The most notable reformationist is Martin Luther, having nailed his 95 Theses to the church door. Luther was a proponent of change in education. He advocated for educational institutions to be open to the common man. It was out of the German, English, and French reformation that we see the creation of a number of universities. As a reminder, disciplines provide a conceptual structure for learning, an instructive community, and a communication network. It was in the late Middle Ages that the term discipline was being applied to theology and arts, law, and medicine. A discipline helps shape the way practitioners see the world. When one pursues disciplinary knowledge, they are learning to see the world through the eyes of its practitioners. For example, if one studies economics, sooner or later they will learn to view the world's phenomena through the concept of supply and demand.

The need for disciplinarity grew out of the demand for specialization, particularly in the legal and medical fields. The first professors were clergymen. Schooled in the discipline of religion, they knew little about medicine. Their practice of medicine was informed by the societal and religious structures of their day. When someone was sick many of these clergymen believed a sick person must have had an evil spirit living inside of them causing the sickness. Methods of healing were born out of the need to cleanse one of an evil spirit. Sometimes they would perform an exorcism. Sometimes they would use leeches to draw contaminated blood from one's body. Sometimes they would drill holes in the head of the sick to release the evil spirit from their mind. The period of enlightenment brought about many changes and in particular changes in the categorization and practice of knowledge. Clearly the medical practices of clergymen in those days did more harm than good. Though there was a greater demand for disciplinary knowledge there was an expressed concern about the fragmentation of knowledge. So there were a number of philosophers that articulated a vision for unity of knowledge (i.e., Kant, Descartes, Hegel, and Comte).

17th and 18th Century Education

In the late 17th and early 18th centuries, the enlightenment aided the growth of disciplines both within and outside of science. The notion that people could find answers to complex problems by means of their reason fostered the view that limiting scholars' fields of inquiry and systematizing knowledge into categories was indispensable to progress. There are some that argue that the fragmentation of knowledge during the enlightenment period was just as harmful. The prototype for the research university that is familiar today was created in Germany in the late 18th century (Frank, 1988). It was meant to provide a liberal or broad education for students, as well as faculty engaged in research. It was this type of university that became the model for which several American universities ultimately reorganized themselves a century or so later. It is the kind of university we primarily see today. Although the power of disciplinary knowledge continued to increase in the 18th century with calls for the non-science to become more scientific, the plethora of disciplines in which we are now familiar did not emerge until the later part of the 19th century. The changes taking place in the concept of knowledge and its delivery to others has been fought over forever. However, by and large the medium for learning and distributing knowledge has been the university; one of the first structured universities dates back to 1088 and the University of Bologna. As the modern university took shape, disciplinarity was reinforced in two major ways: 1) industries demanded and received specialists and 2) disciplines recruited students to their ranks. So, a way was paved for the professionalization of knowledge in the 20th century; history in 1884, economics in 1885, political sciences in 1903, and sociology in 1905.

Interdisciplinarity in 20th Century Education

Since the early 1920s, between 1919 and 1929, new schools and institutions for social science research called for the integration of social sciences and related parts of industry, government, and public welfare. In the 1920s, the Social Science Research Council was established to promote and integrate across disciplines that were being increasingly isolated by specialization (Frank, 1988). George Ellory Hale was the first president of the National Research Council. He discussed the subjects lying between the old established divisions of sciences. One way to conceptualize a discipline is by placing its applicable knowledge inside a box. You have heard the phrase, "think outside the box," right? A discipline is all the knowledge inside of a box. Considering what lies between them is one way to conceptualize interdisciplinarity or synthesizing/integration of those two disciplines or those two systems of knowledge.

It was becoming increasingly apparent that many problems in the post-war period were larger than the scope of any one discipline among them: war, labor, propaganda, population shifts, housing, social welfare, and crime. If you consider what was going on in the 1920s and 1930s, all our men were going to war, they were going to World War I and World War II. As many of the men left the country for the war, women became the labor force in America. More and more women entering the labor force changed the division of labor in the household. Who would take care of the children? Who would take care of the daily functioning of the home? These kinds of changes persisted in our society and have raised many interdisciplinary questions about labor force, gender roles, household duties, and the general definition of family (Hochschild & Machung, 2012). As societies changed with time the notion that we can no longer look at a problem from one perspective became important.

There were a number of terms and a number of ways that people described the idea or concept of interdisciplinarity. The most popular term in books published between 1925 and 1930 for interdisciplinary work was called Cooperative Research. In the 1960s and 70s interdisciplinarity was innovative in higher education. There were interdisciplinarians arguing for the unification of knowledge; we need to know more about more, to solve complex issues and problems in our society. Furthermore, interdisciplinarity was being funded by a number of agencies like the National Science Foundation, Carnegie Foundation, and the National Endowment for the Humanities (NEH), foundation for the improvement of post-secondary education. Frank (1988) noted that interior designers were actually the most fervent interdisciplinarians of the 1970s because they were utilizing multiple disciplines or perspectives to do their work.

The idea of synthesizing knowledge can be seen in the practice of most doctoral programs. In fact, that is why academicians earn Ph.D.s or Doctors of Philosophy, because their task is to synthesize multiple knowledges to add something new and unique to the body of knowledge that exists. Philosophy is considered the branch of knowledge that brings all other knowledges together.

You will find that all universities are organized by college, and within each college there are departments that are organized by a conceptual structure or a system of knowledge. In modern day universities, departments became the channels through which academic resources flowed.

University departments combined with new journals, some of them published by departments, some by disciplinary societies, became the arbiters of academic quality. The disciplinarians became the people who decided what was good and purposeful knowledge and that which was not. They might have posited that certain knowledge is meaningful and other knowledge is not and knowledge which is not meaningful is not considered truthful. For example, consider the argument for the creative design of the world over evolution. One group of disciplinarians, those that think "inside the box," are saying there was a creator, there was a creative design for the world, established by an intelligent designer; nothing else matters to this group. Likewise, another group of disciplinarians think "inside the box"; these disciplinarians, argue that there is no scientific knowledge to support an intelligent designer, a master creator. An interdisciplinarian might ask what does each discipline have to offer that might explain the creation of our world?

Klein discusses the emergence of interdisciplinarity and four ways the modern concept has been shaped. First, by attempts to retain and in many cases reinstall historical ideas of unity and synthesis. Knowledge should be unified not fragmented by the siloing of disciplinary knowledge. da Vinci was not called an interdisciplinarian. However, knowing what we know about interdisciplinarians, we might label him as such; he had a unity of knowledge from multiple fields of study. Secondly, by the emergence of organized programs in research and education. Thirdly by broadening of traditional disciplines. And fourthly, by the emergence of identifiable interdisciplinarity movements like the association for interdisciplinary studies as an organization.

Interdisciplinary programs at universities are becoming increasingly popular. Today, many programs in colleges and universities across the nation, across the world, in fact, have an interdisciplinary degree that would be helpful for students. It is not just academic programs that are becoming increasingly interdisciplinary. You will also find many interdisciplinary, integrative, and transdisciplinary research groups and agendas across many universities and government organizations around the world.

As we wrap up this chapter, consider again the aim of interdisciplinarity that is to construct a more comprehensive perspective or understanding of complex problems and issues utilizing multiple disciplinary insights. Klein and Newell discuss five characteristics of interdisciplinary studies. It is a means for addressing complex problems and issues. It draws from multiple disciplinary perspectives, works towards integration, and constructs a more comprehensive understanding. Finally, it results in correcting and complimenting disciplinary approaches. Full interdisciplinarity requires all five of those characteristics. Partial interdisciplinarity requires at least one element of full interdisciplinarity.

References

Cherniss, H. F. (1944). *Aristotle's criticism of Plato and the academy*. Baltimore: The Johns Hopkins Press.

Cross, R. C. (1964). *Plato's republic* (Vol. 14): New York: St. Martin's Press.

Frank, R. (1988). Interdisciplinary: The first half century. *Issues in Integrative Studies, 6,* 91–101.

Gunn, G. (1992). Interdisciplinary studies. *Introduction to scholarship in modern languages and literatures*, 239–261.

Hochschild, A., & Machung, A. (2012). *The second shift: Working families and the revolution at home*. New York, NY: Penguin.

Klein, J. T. (1990). *Interdisciplinarity: history, theory, & practice*. Detroit, MI: Wayne State University Press.

Newell, W. H. (1998). Professionalizing interdisciplinarity: Literature review and research agenda. *Interdisciplinarity: Essays from the literature*, 529–563.

CHAPTER 3

Theories of Interdisciplinarity & Integrative Learning

Now that we understand a little more about where academic disciplines, interdisciplinarity, and integrative learning originate from, we should explore different theoretical approaches applicable to interdisciplinarity and integrative learning. First, as with most research, there is no one theoretical approach that is more useful than any other for interdisciplinary research or integrative learning. Newell (1983) argues that unanimous agreement of any one theory of interdisciplinarity is not possible and may not even be a desirable goal for interdisciplinarians. However, a consensus on general principles and methods of interdisciplinarity may provide the study of this area with a greater legitimacy. The purpose of this chapter is to present several theories that could be useful as you engage in interdisciplinarity or integrative learning. You should also keep in mind that interdisciplinary research is a process of synthesizing or bringing together multiple disciplinary insights in order to solve a complex problem. The assumption then is that we might also bring together multiple theoretical insights as part of the interdisciplinary research process. Integrative learning is a method by which one can synthesize or bring together multiple contexts as a way to apply interdisciplinarity to complex problems or situations (Hughes, et. al, 2015). Remember, interdisciplinarity requires complexity. Problems that require an interdisciplinary perspective are complex, not easily understood or solved through the theories, methods, or insights of one discipline. In this chapter, we will discuss several theoretical approaches that may be useful to you as you engage in interdisciplinarity and integrative learning. In addition, although we will discuss more fully the interdisciplinary research process in a future chapter, we will introduce several relevant interdisciplinary processes here. We will also discuss several relevant learning theories.

A theory is a set of generalized statements that help us understand "interrelated phenomena and predict behavior or attitudes that are likely to occur when certain conditions are met" (Schutt, 2006, p. 69). Theories are supported by research and its subsequent data. Interdisciplinarians need a basic understanding of relevant theories for several reasons. First, to utilize and integrate disciplinary insights one must know and understand the theories and epistemology of the field.

Second, having a good grasp of a discipline's theories will help you understand their preferred methods of research (Repko, 2013). Interdisciplinarians should be discerning when it comes to accepting evidence for a theory because disciplines choose methods that support their theories (Szostak, 2004). When we think of theories that might be useful to interdisciplinarians, we might consider grand theories, theories that are framed systemically, and learning theories. Grand theories are those that integrate concepts of sociology, psychology, economics, politics, and philosophy. Some examples of grand theory are critical theory and structuralism.

Grand Theories

Critical Theory

As already mentioned, a theory is a set of concepts that helps us understand or explain phenomena of any kind. Certainly, as interdisciplinarians, we want to understand or explain complex problems but perhaps more than that, we need to be able to carefully evaluate one discipline's perspective of a complex problem. Interdisciplinarians assert that interdisciplinarity is needed in order to understand and solve a complex problem; likewise disciplinarians believe their theories and methods are enough. Critical theory may provide some framework for integrative learning and interdisciplinary research. Critical theory critiques and works toward changing societies. Perhaps, Michel Foucault is most notable for using critical theory as a way to work within sociological terms, yet critiques the social or human sciences in an attempt to remain outside the disciplinary frames of inquiry.

There are two core concepts essential to critical theory. First, it is directed toward society as a whole in its historical context. In other words, this concept of critical theory is interested in how a society came to be formed at a specific point in time. Second, critical theory works toward improving the understanding of society by synthesizing all the major social science disciplines (e.g., geography, economics, sociology, history, political science, anthropology, and psychology). An interdisciplinarian may argue that including all the disciplines is not necessary, rather using only those that provide relevant insight into a particular complex problem.

Postmodern critical theory politicizes social problems "by situating them in historical and cultural contexts, to implicate themselves in the process of collecting and analyzing data, and to relativize their findings" (Lindlof and Taylor, 2010, p. 52). The continuing and rapid transformation of societal structures creates difficulty with meaning-making. Thus, the focus of critical theory researchers is directed toward local manifestations of problems rather than broad generalizations. Postmodern critical research is also characterized by the crisis of representation. Crisis of representation refers to the "uncertainty within the human sciences about adequate means of describing social reality" (Schwandt, 2007). Instead, many postmodern scholars have adopted "alternatives that encourage reflection about the 'politics and poetics' of their work. In these accounts, the embodied, collaborative, dialogic, and improvisational aspects of qualitative research are clarified" (Lindlof and Taylor, 2010, p. 53).

Structuralism

Structuralism is a way of thinking about the world as well as a methodology concerned with identifying and describing the structures of societies that cannot be observed only inferred. It is a theory predominately influenced by phenomenology and of Gestalt psychology (Sturrock, 2008, p. 47). Phenomenology is the study of essences or the study of structures of experience and consciousness (see Husserl, Heidegger, Sartre, etc.). Its principle concept is concerned with accurately describing consciousness between subject and object of human thought. Consciousness cannot be separated from the object or the subject rather it is the relationship between them (Sturrock 2008, pp. 50–51). Gestalt psychology posits all human conscious experience is patterned, emphasizing that the whole is always greater than the parts, making it a holistic view (Sturrock 2008). Its principle concept is understanding our ability to acquire and maintain meaningful perceptions in a chaotic work.

Structuralism was developed as a theoretical framework in anthropology by Claude Levi-Strauss. He proposed that cultures, viewed as systems, are analyzed in terms of structural relationship between their parts. Strauss argued that underlying patterns in cultural systems are products of human thought (McGee and Warms, 2004). He proposed that culture is composed of hidden rules that govern the behavior. These hidden rules comprise the differences and uniqueness of cultures. These hidden rules were understood by the people but were difficult to articulate. In anthropology, the goal was to find the meaning of these hidden rules or structures.

For interdisciplinarians, this concept is important for several reasons. First, we might consider a relevant discipline to our research a culture. In this culture there exists underlying patterns of thought, language, rules, and relationships. Framing your interdisciplinary research or integrative learning as a structuralist would lead you to discover, as an anthropologist might, the structure and hidden reality that exists beneath the cultural expressions of a particular discipline. Secondly, a structuralist framework might better help us understand the elements of a particular discipline in terms of their relationship to the entire system (Rubel and Rosman, 1996). The notion, that the whole is greater than the parts, that the elements of culture are not explanatory but instead form part of a meaningful system.

Systemic Theories

Complex Systems Theory

As previously discussed, both interdisciplinarity and integrative learning require complexity as a necessary condition. In other words if a problem or system is not complex, interdisciplinarity and integrative learning are not required. To justify an interdisciplinary approach, its objective study must be multifaceted. Yet its facets must cohere, they must be related to each other in some way. If it is multifaceted but not coherent, then a disciplinary or multidisciplinary approach will be fine for whatever problem or issue one might be studying. Newell (2001) provided justification for using Complex Systems Theory for interdisciplinary studies. Complex systems theory "cuts across the boundaries between conventional scientific disciplines. It makes use of ideas, methods and examples from many disparate fields" (Wolfram, 1988 p. 496).

Newell posits that "interdisciplinarians can better understand and carry out our craft if they keep in mind that they are developing specific complex systems and studying their behavior" (2001, p. 3). Interdisciplinary study is meant to produce a new understanding of a complex problem by synthesizing insights from multiple disciplinary perspectives. Interdisciplinary study facilitates fundamental critique because interdisciplinarians are, characteristically, critical thinkers. They ask good questions about a phenomenon or experience as a way to construct meaningful questions and explore a complex phenomenon or issue. It reduces the pressure for needing a complete understanding of each disciplinary insight. As we will discover in a future chapter, most times it is important that interdisciplinarians have an adequate or working knowledge of the disciplines we are utilizing in our study. It is not necessary to be an expert in a particular discipline.

If so, then Complex Systems Theory may be a good theoretical approach to help us frame our interdisciplinary research process. Thinking of behavior as part of a complex system, for example, may provide an understanding of complex phenomena. We can ask ourselves the following questions: 1) Is it generated by an iterative of solutions of a single equation or by nonlinear relationships? 2) Do the components of a complex system produce an overall pattern of behavior? Does that pattern in turn shape components? 3) Is a pattern merely self-organizing or is it also self-perpetuating (Newell, 2001)? Complex systems are composed of the components actively connected through predominantly nonlinear relationships and so interdisciplinarians would look at multiple connections that exist within a system and in these relationships and then ask meaningful questions. We are looking for a pattern, for connections. Complex systems are self-organizing, self-correcting, self-replicating and so the theoretical approach may be useful as we implement interdisciplinary research process in order to solve a complex problem or issue.

Ecological Systems Theory

Ecology is the study of interrelationships between organisms and the environment, both organic and inorganic. It assumes that life and the environment are inseparable parts of a greater whole.

Ecological systems theory is predicated on the principle that "behavior evolves as a function of the interplay between person and environment" (Bronfenbrenner, 1979, p. 16) and views the development of a person within a "system of relationships affected by multiple levels of the surrounding environment" (Berk, 2008, p. 19).

Bronfenbrenner (1979) posited the ecological environment as a complex system of concentric structures. These structures characterized as the bioecological model (Bronfenbrenner & Evans, 2000) are referred to as the microsystem, mesosystem, exosystem, and macrosystem (see Figure 3.1) (Bronfenbrenner, 1979). The microsystem is the innermost level consisting of bidirectional relationships between an individual and a given setting. The microsystem could be a family home, school, a neighborhood, or a church. We might consider the complex problem of child welfare using ecological systems theory. Using this theory, a child develops through the interaction between themselves and their environment. We need to consider what is happening

FIGURE 3.1   Model of Bronfenbrenner's Ecological Systems

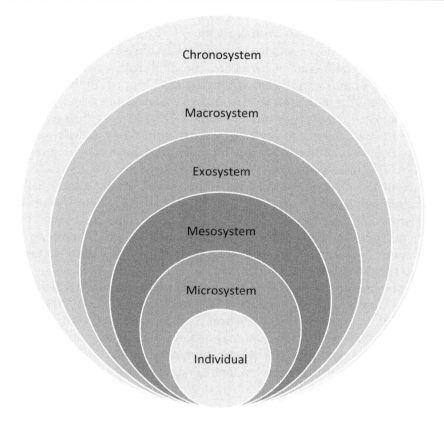

with the child's development as a result of the bidirectional relationship with the microsystem. Much more than that, we need to consider the other levels of the child's ecological system. We will want to know how current child welfare laws promote or prohibit health development. Do public policies help children who are living in poverty rise to and achieve a level of ecological sustainability? Do public policies have a negative effect on children in poverty? What are likely outcomes for children living in poverty? To answer these questions and others, we need to understand more about the nature of each level of a child's environment.

The mesosystem is the second level in the structure and is the interrelations of the microsystems in which a person actively participates. In other words the mesosystem is "a system of microsystems" (p. 25). For children the mesosystem could be the relationship between the school and the family home. There may also be interconnections of other people who actively participate in both settings. One example might be a social worker who is involved in a child's educational system, ensuring they are at school, completing homework, etc. The social worker may also be involved in the home, ensuring the child is in a safe environment, has food and other basic necessities. The child is also participating in each system, thus has interconnections. So not only is there an interaction between the person and different systems but also an interconnection between the person, other persons, and microsystems.

The exosystem is made up of one or more settings in which a person does not actively participate but is affected by influences in that system. An example here might be new or expiring laws of the federal or a state's child welfare laws. The child may not actively participate in the legislation of such laws but is nevertheless affected by what happens in this part of the system.

The macrosystem is the outermost level of the bioecological model and "refers to consistencies, in the form and content of lower-order systems . . . that exist, at the level of the subculture or the culture as a whole, along with any belief systems or ideology underlying such consistencies" (p. 26). To consider a child's welfare, we must consider the overarching values and beliefs of the child, the child's microsystem, mesosystem, and exosystem. Conflict in the macrosystem may have a detrimental effect on the child's development. For example, there have been several reports of children dying or being severely hurt because of the religious values and beliefs of their parents. Some of these values and beliefs contradict the values and beliefs of the American justice system, other cultures, and many in the general public. For example, a young girl died from diabetic shock because the parents refused to administer her insulin. It was their belief that prayer could heal their daughter of diabetes.

Finally, Bronfenbrenner presents the idea of ecological transition in which a person's position in the system shifts as a result of changes in the microsystem (Berk, 2008; Bronfenbrenner, 1979). Relocation is an example of an ecological transition. Again considering a child who is living in poverty, as time goes on, the child may be forced to live in multiple homes, with multiple families, and attend multiple schools. Bronfenbrenner (1979) argues that these transitions are "a consequence and an instigator of developmental processes" (p. 27).

Learning Theories

Experiential Learning Theory

If you have ever taken a course in education, psychology, or sociology, you have probably heard of Kolb's (2012) theory of experiential learning. This is a learning theory that may be useful to you as you engage in integrative learning or interdisciplinarity. According to Kolb, individuals learn as they progress through four stages. Individuals may begin at any stage but they must follow each other in sequence. So for example, you maybe be presented with a complex problem or issue. Then you observe what is taking place concerning the issue. You think about it, you plan to do something about it and then you do it. Take a look at Figure 3.2.

Kolb's learning cycle shows how experiences translated through reflection into concepts which in turn were used as guides for active experimentation and the choice of a new experience. Again, interdisciplinarians make use of multiple perspectives, multiple sources of information, synthesize it, then integrate it into the context of a particular situation. So the first stage in Kolb's theory is this idea of concrete experience. It is where learners actively experience

FIGURE 3.2   Kolb's Experiential Learning Theory

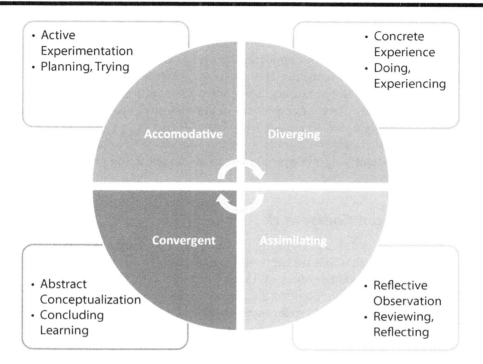

an activity such as a lab, a session, or field work. Then the second stage is reflective observation, where the learner continuously reflects back on that experience. The third stage, abstract conceptualization, is where the learner attempts to conceptualize a theory or model of what is observed and then finally in the fourth stage, active experimentation, is where the learner attempts to plan how to test a model or a theory or plan for forthcoming experiences. Kolb identified four learning styles which correspond to each stage of the process. The styles highlight conditions under which students learn better. The styles are: assimilators, who learn better when presented with sound logical theories to consider; the convergers, who learn better when provided with practical application of concepts and theories; the accommodators, who learn better when provided with hands on experiences; the divergers, who learn better when allowed to observe and collect a wide range of information.

Integrative Learning

Integrative learning is a process where students bridge curricular and co-curricular activities, explore and make connections across their general education curriculum and their major focus of study, and synthesize previous learning with new. Leonard (2012) recently published her theory on how students integrate their learning. Through Leonard's research, she discovered four forms of integration that students engaged in—application, comparison, understanding context, and synthesis where students applied what they were learning to multiple contexts. Students who engaged in synthesis were comparing ideas, concepts, and knowledge, looking at the similarities and differences of two ideas, theories or experiences, and then applying that information to new contexts. Consider the interdisciplinary and integrative nature of what Leonard is discussing; the ability to understand multiple and different contexts and then using synthesis as a way to blend different perspectives to improve one's own understanding. Students in the Leonard study attempted to engage in different forms of integration. She found there were several activities that helped promote integration of multiple areas of study; engaging in relevant coursework, identifying multiple perspectives, encountering conflict, and reconciling conflict.

Engaging in Relevant Coursework

Students who were successful at integrating multiple areas of study were those who engaged in relevant coursework. What that meant for the participants in her study was, first, they were able to articulate the personal relevancy of a topic. In other words, when students were asked to write about any topic, they were able to discover or create ways in which it would be relevant to their personal lives. Secondly, the relevancy was described in terms of connection. Not only were students able to consider topics as relevant to their lives but they were able to describe specific connections to their own experiences. Remember that integration, whether we discuss this term in the context of interdisciplinarity or learning, is about finding the connections between multiple perspectives. I can still remember myself as an undergraduate student, constantly challenging myself to think about how to apply every assignment I completed to my life or to another course I was taking. It was one of the best ways to engage in my coursework. In fact, when I was completing my doctorate one of the best pieces of advice I received from one of my professors was to make an attempt at using every class assignment towards writing my dissertation. If I would engage in such a practice, by the time I got to the dissertation I would have the majority of my literature review completed. Every course I took, whether it was a theory class, a method class, or some particular subject, as part of my doctoral program, I wrote those papers towards my dissertation project. By the time I was ready to write my dissertation I had the majority completed. Engaging in the course work I was taking and attempting to connect it to what I was doing in my other courses was so beneficial. Professors cannot create all of these connections for students, so it is important that interdisciplinary students learn to do this on their own. Leonard also discovered that by engaging in relevant coursework, students contributed to learning self-understanding and self-knowledge. In other words, they engaged in a lot of self-reflection about their learning, what was important about integration, and how they would integrate what they were learning into different contexts.

Identifying Multiple Perspectives

Leonard also discussed students who were able to identify multiple perspectives as they were engaging in coursework were clearly able to consider the value of more than one perspective on any given topic. Leonard provided the following quote from a student participant in the study:

> because even if you are an economics major. Economics is about race, class and gender and media and colonization and globalization. So how can you just study economics and not take classes on or courses in race and gender class and the differences (p. 57).

In this study, it was important that students, even though they were in an economics class, understood that Economics was about other things; thus they were able to take multiple perspectives in integrating into the learning of economics.

Encountering Conflict

Interdisciplinary students also encounter conflicts along the way. When I teach a class on interdisciplinarity or integrative learning, one thing I find fascinating is to observe the behavior of other students when one student discusses their view on what we call a "hot topic," or controversial topic. For example, everyone has an opinion on gay marriage and relationships. Some support it, some are against it, and some are neutral as long as it does not affect them in one way or another. Almost all of the student opinions are very strongly discussed in class. They may have no basis for their opinion or belief but they feel strongly about it nonetheless. People in general have strong opinions about this controversial topic; so do interdisciplinarians. They encounter conflict with their own views and their own beliefs, as well as those of others, when they are challenged to consider opposing views. Many times this conflict occurs based on the values and beliefs of their raising not necessarily from critically considering and supporting what their own viewpoint may be. So through encountering conflict and critical thinking the participants in Leonard's project were able to see another's perspective; they were able to find common ground and then create a new understanding of a complex issue. Encountering conflict is important for the interdisciplinarian. When students in the Leonard study encountered conflict, they would engage in debate but would ultimately view the conflict as positive to their learning experience. This idea is important for interdisciplinarians and integrative learners, to view debates and the differences of opinion as positive because the point is to purposefully look for those differences then find the common ground; find the connection for a new way to understand the problem.

Conflict within self is something else that participants engaged in or experienced in Leonard's project. Whether it was private or public conflicting with personal views, conflict created discomfort, but it was beneficial. Students would leave class and think about the debate privately. Even outside of the debate, they were thinking about other viewpoints. They may not express that consideration publicly, but privately they were thinking about what was going on thus engaging in a synthesis of learning.

Reconciling Conflict

Beyond encountering conflict, interdisciplinarians must learn to reconcile conflict. Interdisciplinary students who are considering a complex or controversial topic will consider multiple perspectives then locate multiple sources of information on this topic. They will find the patterns and connections or common ground and ultimately the goal is to create a new understanding of the problem; resolving the conflict between the multiple perspectives. Interdisciplinary students might work together to reconcile conflict, working in teams, for example, another characteristic of interdisciplinarians. Interdisciplinarians would reduce their own discomfort about a controversial topic, reconciling internal or external conflict, by synthesizing or integrating the multiple perspectives of their team.

Interdisciplinary Research Process

As we have already discussed, interdisciplinary research is an approach to studying a complex problem. The interdisciplinary research process attempts to integrate the disciplinary insights of more than one relevant discipline and construct a more comprehensive understanding of the complex problem. Additionally, I have already stated that there is no one theoretical approach to interdisciplinary research. Even within the field of interdisciplinarity, scholars have some disagreement on the process. Klein, Newell, Soztak, and Repko have all published a process for engaging in interdisciplinary research. Repko's ten step process is the most cited by most interdisciplinarians. However, Repko published a 10-step process for interdisciplinary research in 2012 and in 2013 published a 6-step process. All of these process models are redundant. Because of this it is difficult to know which process students should engage and use. Is one process better than any other? I do not believe so, but it can be confusing for students. So we will present three of the most cited processes here then integrate them into a five-step process in an effort for parsimony. So here are Klein's (1990) 12 steps of the interdisciplinary research process:

1. Define the problem
2. Determine all knowledge needs
3. Develop an integrative framework and appropriate questions to be investigated
4. Specify particular studies to be undertaken
5. Engage in role negotiation (Teamwork)
6. Gather all current knowledge and search for new information
7. Resolve disciplinary conflicts

8. Build and maintain communication through integrative techniques
9. Collate all contributions and evaluate their adequacy
10. Integrate the individual pieces to determine a pattern
11. Confirm or disconfirm the proposed solutions
12. Decide about future management of the task

Newell (2001) looks at the process through 13 steps instead of 12, but as you can see his process is very similar to Klein's.

1. Define the problem
2. Determine relevant disciplines
3. Develop working command of relevant concepts, theories, methods of each discipline
4. Gather all current disciplinary knowledge and search for new information
5. Study the problem from the perspective of each discipline
6. Generate disciplinary insights into the problem
7. Identify conflicts in insights
8. Evaluate assumptions and terminology
9. Resolve conflicts by working towards a common vocabulary
10. Create common ground
11. Construct a new understanding of the problem
12. Produce a model that captures the new understanding
13. Test the understanding by attempting to solve the problem

Repko (2012) provides a process model for doing interdisciplinary research. He outlines his model as a 10-step process:

1. Define the problem or state the research question
2. Justify using an interdisciplinary approach
3. Identify relevant disciplines
4. Conduct the literature search
5. Develop adequacy in each relevant discipline
6. Analyze the problem and evaluate each insight or theory
7. Identify conflicts between insights or theories and their sources
8. Create common ground between concepts and theories
9. Construct a more comprehensive understanding
10. Reflect on, test, and communicate the understanding

You will notice a lot of redundancy with each of the above processes of interdisciplinarity. Not to create yet another list for you but rather in an attempt to synthesize this information, I have provided you with a five-step process below.

1. Define a complex issue or problem. Be specific and provide background information concerning the issue/problem.
2. Justify an interdisciplinary approach. What meaningful questions can you ask about the issue/problem? How are these questions interdisciplinary? What makes them meaningful?
3. Locate multiple sources of relevant disciplinary knowledge, information, and perspectives that will address the issue/problem.
4. Critically analyze common disciplinary insights, conflicts, and patterns of connection.
5. Create and discuss an integrative framework that provides for a holistic understanding of the issue/problem.

There are several important concepts that are important to the interdisciplinary research process. The first is common ground. Common ground was first introduced as an interdisciplinary concept by Newell (2001) as involving various techniques that modify or reinterpret disciplinary insights. This particular concept is what makes integration possible. Repko (2013) defined common ground as "that which is created between conflicting disciplinary insights, assumptions, concepts, or theories and makes integration possible" (p. 131). The second concept important to the interdisciplinary process is interdisciplinary integration. Repko (2013) defines interdisciplinary integration as "the cognitive process of critically evaluating disciplinary insights and creating common ground among them to construct a more comprehensive understanding. The new understanding is the product or result of the integrative process" (p. 133).

The theories and processes we have discussed in this chapter help provide a framework for understanding interdisciplinarity and integrative learning. But what do interdisciplinarians see within that frame? In the next chapter, we will discuss the epistemology of interdisciplinary studies as well the very important concept of critical thinking.

References

Berk, L. (2008). *Exploring lifespan development*. Boston: Pearson Education Inc.

Bronfenbrenner, U. (1979). *The ecology of human development: Experiments by nature and design*. Boston: Harvard University Press.

Bronfenbrenner, U., & Evans, G. W. (2000). Developmental science in the 21st century: Emerging questions, theoretical models, research designs and empirical findings. *Social Development, 9*(1), 115–125. doi:10.1111/1467-9507.00114

Hughes, P. C., Munoz, J. S., & Tanner, M. N. (Eds.). (2015). *Perspectives on Interdisciplinary and Integrative Studies*. Lubbock, TX: Texas Tech University Press.

Klein, J. T. (1990). The interdisciplinary process. *International research management*, 20–30.

Kolb, A. Y., & Kolb, D. A. (2012). Experiential learning theory. In Seel, N. (Ed.), *Encyclopedia of the Sciences of Learning* (pp. 1215–1219). New York: Springer.

Leonard, J. B. (2012). Integrative learning: A grounded theory. *Issues in Integrative Studies 30*, 48–74.

Lindlof, T. R., & Taylor, B. C. (2010). *Qualitative communication research methods*. Thousand Oaks, CA: Sage.

Newell, W. H. (1983). The case for interdisciplinary studies. *Issues in Integrative Studies, 2*, 1–19.

Newell, W. H. (2001). A theory of interdisciplinary studies. *Issues in Integrative Studies, 19*, 1–25.

Repko, A. F. (2012). *Interdisciplinary research: Process and theory* (2nd ed.). Thousand Oaks, CA: Sage Publications, Inc.

Repko, A. F., Szostak, R. R., & Buchberger, M. P. (2013). *Introduction to interdisciplinary studies*. Thousand Oaks, CA: Sage.

Schutt, R. K. (2006). *Investigating the social world: The process and practice of research* (5th ed.) Newbury Park, CA: Pine Forge Press.

Schwandt, T. A. (2007). *The Sage dictionary of qualitative inquiry*. Thousand Oaks, CA: Sage.

Sturrock, J. (2003). *Structuralism: With an Introduction by Jean-Michel Rabate* (2nd ed.). Hoboken, NJ: Wiley-Blackwell.

Szostak, R. (2004). *Classifying science: Phenomena, data, theory, method, practice* (Vol. 7). Thousand Oaks, CA: Springer.

Wolfram, S. (1988). Cellular automaton supercomputing. In R. B. Wilhelmson (Ed.), *High-Speed Computing: Scientific Applications and Algorithm Design* (pp. 40–48). University of Illinois Press.

CHAPTER 4

Epistemology and Critical Thinking

"The concept of interdisciplinarity is rooted in the ideals of a unity and synthesis of knowledge and general education, ideals that, according to George Gusdorf, have been reinvented again and again, throughout the history of the pursuit if knowledge: "the ideal of knowledge of one single realm is a constant factor in epistemology" (1977, p. 581 in Klein, 1990).

Critical thinking is the mental process of actively and skillfully conceptualizing, applying, analyzing, synthesizing, and evaluating information to reach an answer or a conclusion. To engage in interdisciplinary or integrative studies one must be a critical thinker. As mentioned in the previous chapter, several theories useful to interdisciplinarians are critical in nature. Meaning it is important to understand that one's disciplinary perspective could not provide the answer(s) or adequately inform our understanding of a complex problem or issue. For example, interdisciplinarians would view the problems of child welfare through the relationship between public policy, psychology, sociology, anthropology, etc. Doing so provides a more holistic understanding of the problem than simply viewing child welfare issues through the disciplinary lens of psychology and mental health.

An interdisciplinarian, a critical thinker, has a number of important characteristics as Ennis (2002) described:

1. Is open-minded and mindful of alternatives
2. Desires to be, and is, well-informed
3. Judges well the credibility of sources
4. Identifies reasons, assumptions, and conclusions
5. Asks appropriate clarifying questions
6. Judges well the quality of an argument, including its reasons, assumptions, evidence, and their degree of support for the conclusion

7. Can well develop and defend a reasonable position regarding a belief or an action, doing justice to challenges

8. Formulates plausible hypotheses

9. Plans and conducts experiments well

10. Defines terms in a way appropriate for the context

11. Draws conclusions when warranted—but with caution

12. Integrates all of the above aspects of critical thinking

Although all of these are important, perhaps standing out as being indispensable for engaging in critical thought is that interdisciplinarians must be open-minded, cognizant of other alternatives. The ability to do this helps us engage in the interdisciplinary research process described in the previous chapter. It is important that we engage in **meta-cognition** or thinking about thinking. It is important that you understand that critical thinkers must be independent thinkers, examining problems and issues for ourselves; unless we examine how we come to know what we know, we forfeit our right to think independently.

When I consider the concept of critical thinking, I am concerned about how little of it people engage in today. We live in a society where information is handed down from authoritative sources, just like I am doing in this textbook. For you to take everything written in this book as true without consideration is not critical thinking.

When I was working full time as a minister, I would often tell the group of people I was speaking to not to take everything I say as truth. Instead, they should go home, read, and study the Scripture for themselves. It was also important to me to welcome appropriate discussion about the topics I was teaching on, because critical thinking is one thing that we learn. To examine important issues, values, and beliefs without taking everything at face value is important in our lives.

Allow me a little more latitude to tell my own story of critical thinking about something important to me. When I began my doctoral program, my critical thinking skills were seriously challenged. All of my life I grew up in a ministry home where my family was very involved in church. My wife grew up in a ministry home; her parents were pastors. The context of our development was within the framework of Christianity and to a greater extent ministry. We were always very involved in church; we grew up in church. I was raised to believe certain truths and concepts about God and man's relationship with Jesus Christ. I was taught that there was only one way to believe and that way was based on the beliefs of the denomination or the church in which we belonged. Many students struggle with their religious faith when they come to college; assuming they have a religious faith when they arrive. What happened to me was the opposite of what happens to many who lose their faith. My religious faith was strengthened because I was challenged to study, on my own, what I valued, my belief system, and how those aligned with my faith in God. The practice of studying on my own challenged me to not simply accept those values and beliefs that were handed down to me by parents, by the church that I was involved in, but I had to figure it out on my own and critically evaluate those value and beliefs.

The ability to critically evaluate disciplinary insights, multiple perspectives, and multiple contexts is important for interdisciplinarians. Susanne Langer (1944) said,

> We live in a mind-made world where the things of prime importance are images or words that embody ideas and feelings and attitudes . . . Language, religion, mathematics, all learning, all sciences and superstition, even right and wrong, are products of symbolic expression rather than direct experience.

It is important for us to ask the right questions. Critical thinking helps us do that. To ask the right questions, better questions, of why do we believe what we believe and how do know presented information is true? Let us now take a look at another important concept to integrative and interdisciplinary studies, epistemology. **Epistemology** is simply this, a way of knowing. It is a branch of philosophy that investigates the origin, nature, methods, and limits of human knowledge. You might ask yourself, "how do I know what I know"? Previously, we discussed the idea that interdisciplinarians seek the knowledge or the epistemologies that lie between the old established divisions of science. Take a look at Figure 4.1 below.

Think of a discipline as a box. In the figure there are three boxes labeled psychology, public policy, and education. You can see that these boxes are separate and there's nothing that connects them. They are just three boxes or three ways of knowing or disciplinary perspectives. As interdisciplinarians we must learn to unpack or critically evaluate the disciplines.

Integrative and interdisciplinary studies engage in epistemological pluralism, which embraces the ambiguity that arises out of conflict and difference. Welch (2011) discussed the idea that knowledge emerges from the cross fertilization of different perspectives. Thus, interdisciplinarians negotiate within and beyond the epistemological frameworks constructed by disciplines. So we need to unpack the disciplinary box, consider its epistemology, culture, behavior, methods, and relationships. If we continue with the example of child welfare and unpacking the boxes, how disciplines might view this complex issue, we first might to consider the discipline of psychology. As we unpack this box, we will want to critically evaluate their epistemology which will in turn help us understand the important and relevant disciplinary insights psychology might have for our child welfare issue. It is important to reiterate here

FIGURE 4.1   Disciplinary Boxes

Psychology   **Public Policy**   **Education**

that interdisciplinarians need not become experts in a particular discipline; it is enough for them to be adequate. Once we have unpacked the disciplinary box of psychology, we would then do the same with public policy and education. We will find their epistemologies or the way that they understand the issue of child welfare is different. The interdisciplinary process helps us locate the knowledge that lies between the old established divisions of science. It is what Latucca (2001) meant when she defined interdisciplinarity as the interaction of different disciplines. As we study the interaction between the epistemologies given a specific complex problem, we can then engage in what we described earlier as finding common ground and interdisciplinary integration.

Petrie (1976) suggested different disciplines look at the same phenomenon but they observe different effects. Take a look at Figure 4.2. What do you see? Most of you will look at this picture and see something different than your classmates.

Some of you see an old woman. The old woman is wearing a scarf and has what appears to be a fur coat. She also has a very large nose. Others of you see a young woman. Her head is slightly turned to the side and the old woman's nose is actually the chin and neckline of the young woman. Where some of you can only see one of the images is one way to view disciplinarity. Disciplinarians can only view the world from their epistemology. Interdisciplinarians on

FIGURE 4.2   Two Face Illusion

Learning from the Gecko

The experiments that the interdisciplinary teams conducted on the gecko are interesting and produce some incredible results. One thing you may not pick up on in the video is one part of the team admits they would have never thought about looking at the problem from a certain perspective without having been asked about it from another part of the team. At some point some of the researchers were looking at the problem from a disciplinary lens instead of an interdisciplinary lens. As you watch the video, see if you can recognize the disciplinary perspectives and the connections the team was able to make. Then see if you can recognize the integration that exists in that video. How did they apply what they were learning?

Image © nico99/Shutterstock, Inc.

http://www.ted.com/talks/robert_full_learning_from_the_gecko_s_tail?language=en.

the other hand, have the ability to see both, the ability to see the world from multiple perspectives or at least know that multiple perspectives exist and can be known.

Why is critical thinking and epistemology important for interdisciplinarians? Why do we need interdisciplinarians? There is a place in this world for specialists, disciplinarians, and interdisciplinarians. The world needs specialists and disciplines. This text is not an argument against the disciplines. Specialists and disciplinarians have provided a great wealth of knowledge to this world. Knowledge that has produced some of the greatest advances our world has ever known. However, we also need interdisciplinarians. Interdisciplinary teams have also produced new ways to understand complex issues and problems in our world. They too have created some of the greatest advances of our world. See the spotlight on Learning from the Gecko for more information on how one team of researchers used questions and knowledge from other disciplines to inform their work.

Worldviews

Epistemology leads us to view the world from a particular perspective. There are several categories of worldviews that are important for us to briefly discuss in this chapter. The first is the notion of modernism, which is that the real world exists independent of our knowledge of it. Within that idea of modernism exists the notions of positivism, realism, behaviorism, rational choice, and Marxism. All of these worldviews fit within the ideology of modernism. Another worldview is interpretivism, which states that the world can be interpreted on an individual basis, but it can never really be known. Individuals can interpret the world in different ways. The interpretation of one individual is not necessarily the interpretation of another individual. Because multiple interpretations of the world can exist it can never be truly known. Postmodernism is another worldview where the world is discursively constructive. Postmodernists are skeptical or suspicious of reason. Postmodernists typically believe that truth is relative or subjective to each individual and their individual context. In other words, what is true for one may not be true for another though all things are equal between them.

Epistemological reflexivity is an examination or testing of assumptions, the analysis of your experience and theoretical and methodological beliefs about your worldview or that of others. Good interdisciplinary work requires epistemological and self-reflexivity. That is to say that interdisciplinarians are constantly asking important questions of ourselves and our work; am I moving in the right direction? Interdisciplinarians discuss and reflect on their lived experiences and the connections between those experiences. Reflexivity involves critically thinking about our limitations, the knowledge we already have, and the knowledge yet to be known. As we write, we reflect on the past and what that means for the future, and what is happening in the present.

References

Ennis, R. H. (2002). A super-streamlined conception of critical thinking. Retrieved January 13, 2015, from http://faculty.ed.uiuc.edu/rhennis

Klein, J. T. (1990). *Interdisciplinarity: history, theory, & practice*. Detroit, MI: Wayne State University Press.

Langer, S. K. (1944, January). The Lord of Creation. *Fortune 29*, 127–154.

Lattuca, L. R. (2001). *Creating interdisciplinarity: Interdisciplinary research and teaching among college and university faculty*. Nashville, TN: Vanderbilt University Press.

Petrie, H. G. (1976). Do you see what I see? The epistemology of interdisciplinary inquiry. *Journal of Aesthetic Education*, 29–43.

Welch IV, J. (2011). The emergence of interdisciplinarity from epistemological thought. *Issues in Integrative Studies, 29*, 1–39.

CHAPTER 5

Integrative Learning

Integrative learning is simply the ability to synthesize learning across various settings and contexts (Huber and Hutching, 2004; Klein, 2005; Newell, 1999). As a student, your ability to do this is critical to your success in most interdisciplinary programs. Integrative learning is not necessarily natural. As you continue to learn more about integrative learning you may come to consider much of it common sense or the way individuals typically operate in this world, but not necessarily. I would argue it is intentional. Carey (2005) says, "integrative learning encourages students to make connections between their new and existing knowledge, skills and experiences which in turn allows them to respond to the changing needs of a society" (p. 3). Integrative learning is a skill that can be applied to more than academic coursework. It is a skill that you can apply to many experiences you might have in life, including your vocation. Students who operate as integrative learners utilize their cognitive reasoning skills in such a way that allows for greater learning and retention to occur, but there are barriers to learning, especially in undergraduate programs. Many times students take courses that do not seem to connect with one another so it is important that they be intentional about finding ways to connect course content and learning across the curriculum. Many times it is up to the student to create an environment where connections might be sought. In some regards, the burden to create integrative learning environments lies with the educator, but the disciplinary structure and constraints of most institutions are prohibitive.

Creating Your Own Integrative Experiences

It is important that students explore opportunities for integrative learning on their campus and how they might create their own integrative experiences. Remember, AAC&U (2004) defines integrative learning as an understanding and a disposition that a student builds across the curriculum or co-curriculum for making simple connections among ideas and experiences to synthesizing and transferring learning to new complex situations within and beyond the campus. At many universities there are many opportunities for undergraduate and graduate students to be engaged in integrative learning, i.e., service learning, interdisciplinary research, study abroad, etc. For example, in service learning courses students are provided the opportunity to synthesize what they are learning in class with experience providing a service to a community partner.

Integrative Learners as Lifelong Learners

The average career lasts 4.4 years (Kamenetz, 2012). Many of you reading this will have three to five careers before you retire. With so many expected changes in the life of your career, integrative and lifelong learning can be beneficial. Consider this, would you want to waste all that you have learned in your first career of one to three years? Perhaps you go on to an unrelated career but you learned some valuable skills previously. Why not consider integrating what you learned during your first career into the second? Everything you learned may not be applicable but there is little doubt you will have acquired some transferable skills. You may also have to create connections between your careers as an integrative learner would. Your transferable skills would be a valuable asset to your employer and consequently to you as you potentially move up through the ranks in your new career. As people are living and working longer, the idea of being an integrative and lifelong learner allows them to become more flexible and mobile in the workplace. As students know more about more and know how to connect those transferable skills from one context to another they can place themselves in a valuable position to potential employers.

As has already been mentioned in this part of the textbook, integrative learners have the ability to weave together the sometimes obscure threads of their life in a way that makes sense. Allow me to illustrate by sharing more of my own experiences. Before I graduated high school I began working in retail and worked in retail for 10 years before changing careers. There was some overlap in my career change as I retooled for pastoral ministry. My career in full-time ministry lasted 12 years. I thought I was going to add more tools to my ministry toolbox when I began my doctoral program; instead I was retooling for another career change. Combining my work as an administrator and teacher, I have been at the university now for seven years. Those are three very different careers. The contexts are very different in retail, ministry, and working at the university. However, as an integrative and lifelong learner, I have been able to pick up skills in retail that were very valuable and transferable to a career in ministry. Likewise, I picked up skills and abilities while working in pastoral ministry that have been very valuable and transferable skills as a teacher and administrator. For interdisciplinarians the notion of integrative and lifelong learning is indispensable. Not only do interdisciplinary and integrative studies help you understand the interdisciplinary research process but their concepts can be applied to almost every area of your life.

The Half Life of Information

Consider this, unless you become intentional about your learning, most of the information you learn at the university or in some other context is going to become useless in a few years. Here is a link to a great video that illustrates the notion of the half-life of information, http://www.youtube.com/watch?v=GaxYnvd7YAM. Lagemann (2003) says,

> One might even venture that vocation broadly defined tends usually to be the thing that links the different experiences that defined and individuals education so think about that as you watch, the information half-life. Integrative learning requires intentionality it requires a deliberateness, a reflexivity. It is this lifelong learning approach beyond the college years.

Responsible Citizenry

It is a very important characteristic for interdisciplinarians to participate responsibly as citizens. Students must be able to synthesize learning from a wide array of sources. Not just from what is learned from years in college, but from the values and beliefs one has as a person, from their experiences at work, personal experiences, relationships, etc. It is important that integrative learners be able to make productive connections between theory and practice. Integrative learners understand how to apply information in a life context. Integrative learning is important because it is greater than the sum of its parts. Integrative and lifelong learners have both a breadth and depth of knowledge in addition to the skills necessary to apply that knowledge to multiple perspectives (see Klein; Newell; and Repko).

Being an integrative and lifelong learner is about educating the whole person, not just one aspect. Integrative learning leads to personal liberation, social empowerment, and inspires and challenges higher education. The concept of critical thinking as an integrative learner is what liberates a person, not to be constrained by prohibitive parameters of institutional structures rather to bridge boundaries, to consider life from multiple perspectives and contexts, synthesizing and applying that knowledge into a new holistic understanding of complex problems and issues one might face.

Central to interdisciplinary scholarship, whether focused on discovery, creativity, or integrating and interpreting knowledge from different disciplines is applying knowledge through real world engagements or teaching students and communicating with the public. It is inspiring and challenging. Integrative and lifelong learning has led many to accomplish great things in this world and in our communities.

Integrative learning also has an emotional appeal. When students become passionate about their learning, whether academic, job related, learning something about relationships, or learning something new about parenting; when one becomes passionate about a topic, it ignites their enthusiasm and integration is more likely to happen. As a student, when you work on being intentional about integrative and lifelong learning, find things that you are passionate about to be involved in and to learn more about. Consider what Huber and Hutching (2004) say about integrative learning, "To participate responsibly as citizens, students must be able to synthesize learning" (p. 4). Students need to develop strategies for connecting their curricular, co-curricular, and life experiences.

Education is a quest not a requirement. It is not such a thing that allows one to simply go through the motions—going to class, writing papers, taking quizzes, get your grades at the end— this is a boring way to educate yourself. You want to make education intentional and that requires work on your part as a student. Your teachers create lectures, lessons, and assignments that hopefully teach and challenge you to learn and retain knowledge. They can present in fun and unique ways but in some ways their task ends there. It is up to you make disparate courses, programs, and disciplinary knowledge relevant to your own education and life. Teachers cannot do that for you.

There are three associated abilities with strategic integrative learning: how to learn, how to conduct the inquiry (e.g., critical thinking and constructing knowledge), and how to be a self-directed learner. Integrative learners develop the skills necessary to seek out information in addition to what is presented in course content, to collect more information about certain topics and concepts, in order to fully grasp information. Consider Ellen Weinstein's (1996) framework for the strategic learner; she says that,

> they need to have knowledge in five broad categories: knowledge about themselves, about different types of academic tasks, about strategies, and methods for acquiring in using new knowledge, about how the prior content knowledge, can be applied. Then finally how the present and future context in which new information can be useful" (pp. 49–50).

Integrative and lifelong learners participate in metacognition and reflective practice. **Metacognition** is defined as knowing about knowing or thinking about thinking. For example, metacognitive activities can be planning on how to approach a given learning task. Metacognition might take the shape of planning how you complete a given assignment, and considering how you might best meet the goals and requirements of the assignment. You might engage in metacognitive activity such as monitoring comprehension, considering whether you were able to grasp a presented concept. If not, consider questions you might ask about the concept. In other words, check for understanding. Metacognition also involves evaluating progress toward the completion of a task. To be a strategic integrative learner, you must create your own goals for your education. Be an active learner; be active in your learning environment.

Be intentional about finding connections between curricular and co-curricular activities. Find the connections between course assignments; discover how you might make them meaningful to you and your career and future plans. Develop explicit learning goals for yourself. Take ownership of your education; write down explicit educational goals. Consider what you want to achieve from your education. As you work toward these goals, be very self-reflective concerning how you will meet those goals and your progress. Consider people you might partner with that can help you achieve these goals; work with your professors and your classmates in order to meet those goals.

Let me end this chapter with one more personal story about the possibilities of integrative learning. I was coming near the end of my career in retail. About the last five years I had been working in loss prevention. Over time, I noticed a trend with certain people. As I investigated these trends, I found that some of these people had elaborate schemes that were costing the company millions of dollars a year. I saw a pattern in their activity, the connection, as I researched their methods. I attempted to combat this problem from different perspectives. One thing I learned was that we did not have the necessary people, skills, or knowledge to curtail these enormous losses. As I continued to learn more about the shoplifting groups, laws, human behavior, and more about the company, I proposed a new position. Although young I was able to work with my superiors, regional vice presidents, and finally the CEO of the company to create a new position for this worldwide company. I was 22 years old at the time. I credit my accomplishment to the interdisciplinary skills and abilities that I had been developing.

I encourage you, as a student, in your career, or life in general, to seek out complex problems. Create integrative learning environments for yourself. Do not take the boring and routine route of education, simply going through the turnstiles; take ownership of your education. Be intentional, self-aware, and purposeful about your education. Finally, let me end this chapter with a quote, "through reflection we surface and criticize the tacit understanding that have grown up around repetitive experiences of specialized practice and can make a new sense of situations of uncertainty or uniqueness" (Schön, 1983 p. 61).

References

AAC&U. (2004). A statement on integrative learning. Retrieved from http://www.aacu.org/integrative_learning/pdfs/ILP_Statement.pdf

Carey, S. J. (2005). From the editor. *Peer Review, 7*(4), 3.

Huber, M. T., & Hutchings, P. (2004). *Integrative learning: Mapping the terrain.* Washington DC: Association of American Colleges and Universities.

Kamenetz, A. (2012). The four year career. Retrieved January 13, 2015, from http://www.fastcompany.com/1802731/four-year-career

Klein, J. T. (2005). Integrative learning and interdisciplinary studies. *Peer Review, 7*(4), 8–10.

Lagemann, E. C. (Spring 2003). The Challenge of Liberal Education: Past, Present, and Future. *Liberal Education, 89*(2).

Newell, W. H. (1999). The Promise of Integrative Learning. *About campus, 4*(2), 17–23.

Schön, D. A. (1983). *The reflective practitioner: How professionals think in action* (Vol. 5126). New York, NY: Basic books.

Weinstein, C. E. (1996). Learning How to Learn: An Essential Skill for the 21st Century. *Educational Record, 66*(4), 49–52.

PART II

Interdisciplinary Research

CHAPTER 6

Basic Research Methods

In order for you to understand the interdisciplinary research process, you will need to have some basic knowledge of disciplinary research methods. Research is the systematic investigation into a phenomenon in order to learn more about the phenomenon and how it is experienced. Although we will define important terms and methods related to disciplinary research methods, this chapter does not provide an exhaustive survey of research methods. Rather, it is meant to provide an overview of basic research methods. In addition to discussing basic research methods in this chapter, this part of the textbook will provide a general overview discussion of the interdisciplinary research process and methods of integration as it relates to the interdisciplinary research process.

Each discipline has its own preferred methods of research consistent with its preferred theories and epistemology. Preferred methods of research are different depending on whether a discipline falls into the category of Science, Social Science, or Humanities. In addition, the research design is primarily dependent on the research question but also relies on ethics, budget, time, and resources. The first thing a researcher does is determine the **research question**, a question about specific phenomena, the social world, event, or written document. Research questions can be developed in different ways. Common sources of questions or problems include existing theories, past research, our own personal experiences, and everyday events.

Everyday life provides a great source of potential research questions. The astute observer might witness an event or a behavior of some sort and ask "Why?" this might have occurred. One's desire to learn more about a particular event or behavior would lead them to investigate further into the matter. Perhaps they would search through or review existing literature on a particular behavior to see what has already been discovered. The **literature review** might highlight a gap in the existing knowledge of a particular behavior. Attempting to fill this gap in the existing knowledge would help us construct our research question. Likewise, practical issues we experience as we live our life might lead us toward a good research question. Everyday life and practical issues are what helped me find my research question while working on my doctorate. Having spent over a decade in pastoral ministry, I saw many of my colleagues experience great stress, burnout, mental and physical health issues, as well financial and family problems. Sometimes these problems were due to stressful work environments or stressful family environments. I also noticed that some of my colleagues would work at a church for a short time then seemingly disappear with no announcement of their leaving. My inquisitive nature led me to ask questions about this phenomena and I discovered many did not want to talk about it. A few years later I discovered personally why my colleagues did not want to share their experiences. There is a phenomenon in the church called forced termination. It is when a church and/or their legislative body, usually the church board, decide they no longer want a minister at their church. Instead of firing them, as would happen in most workplaces, they psychologically and sometimes physically abuse the minister and sometimes their family until they are forced to leave. Wanting to understand my own experiences with this phenomenon and those of others I knew, I began looking for past research. Finding none, I knew there was a very large gap in the existing literature.

You might look through previous research on a particular topic of interest to you. As you review past research you may come across interesting findings or conclusions but the researcher never followed up on the findings. You might also find research that you disagree with and want to investigate whether or not the findings of a previous researcher still hold true. You might also find good research questions within existing theories. Remember, a theory helps us understand or explain a phenomenon. Perhaps you find a theory that helps you understand almost all there is to know about the relationship between parent and child, but you have experienced or observed some unique behavior that is not explained by a particular theory. Are there other theories that do explain it? If not, you might be able to extend the current theory by further explaining the unique behavior.

Once you have determined your research question as well your budget, resources, and ethical implications, your question will inform what kind of research you will do. There are different kinds of research, and each has methods that are more appropriate. For example, perhaps your research question leads you to investigate an area that has not been researched or is very under-researched. You might then engage in **descriptive research** where the purpose of your study is to collect data and make generalizations about your findings. Much of my early research has been descriptive in nature because there is almost no research in my current specific area of focus. Perhaps you already have some data that might be used for **inductive research**, where you develop an explanation of the data. **Exploratory research** is inductive and often uses qualitative research methods. Your research question might lead you to design a test to explain specific phenomena. **Explanatory research** uses **deductive reasoning** to test these explanations. Another type of explanatory research is **evaluative research,** which seeks to, for example, determine the effects of public policies (Schutt, 2006).

Depending on the type of research your research question leads you to do you might decide to use a specific category of research design that best suits your question. Although there are others we will briefly define and discuss four categories of research design. First, many research designs you will come across are **quantitative**, information based on numbers. Quantitative methods rely on surveys and experiments to record variation in the subject of study. It is the standard experimental method of most scientific disciplines and many social sciences. Scientists who work to protect their disciplinary territory claim this method as the only true scientific method as it uses traditional mathematical and statistical reasoning to measure results.

You may also come across very important research studies that used a qualitative method. **Qualitative methods** involve studying participants or things in their natural environment. These methods explore and interpret the meaning individuals assign to phenomena and is characterized by participant observation, intense interviewing, focus groups, rich narrative descriptions, is process oriented, and involves inductive data analysis (Schutt, 2006; Trumbull, 2005).

There is also a category of research design called a mixed method approach. A **mixed method** approach "uses quantitative and qualitative methods, either concurrently (i.e., independent of each other) or sequentially (e.g., findings from one approach inform the other), to understand a phenomenon of interest" (Venkatesh, Brown, & Bala, 2013). The fourth category of research design is the case study. A **case study** "is an empirical inquiry that investigates a contemporary phenomenon within its real life context, especially when the boundaries between phenomenon and context are not clearly evident" (Yin, 1994, p. 13). Case studies are not really a category of method but a way of thinking about qualitative data analysis (Schutt, 2006).

Depending on the category of method your research question guides you toward, you may have different goals in mind for the research project. You may also utilize different specific methods whether you use a quantitative or qualitative approach. The next several sections of this chapter will be devoted to defining and discussing specific research methods associated with the four categories discussed above.

Research Goals

Whether you are a scientist, social scientist, or one who investigates the humanities, and whether you use a quantitative, qualitative, mixed method, or case study approach, you will have different goals in mind as you construct your research instrument. Researchers might first be concerned with **validity**, when our statements or conclusions about an empirical reality are correct (Schutt, 2006). There are four types of validity we should be concerned with as we engage in research; statistical validity, construct validity, internal validity, and external validity (Christensen, Johnson, & Turner, 2011). Especially in quantitative research we are also concerned with measurement validity; that is, "the extent to which any measuring instrument measures what is intended to measure" (Cronbach, 1971, p. 447).

Another aspect of validity we should be concerned with is generalizability, "the degree to which the findings can be generalized from the study sample to the entire population" (Polit & Hungler, 1991, p. 645, as cited in Myers, 2000). Good research should be generalizable to a specific population, group, setting, or phenomena given specific conditions outlined in the research. We should also be concerned with **causal validity** (or **internal validity**) that the independent and dependent variables are causally related (Christensen, Johnson, & Turner, 2011, p. 169), and **authenticity,** which is "reflecting fairly the perspectives of participants in a setting that we study" (Schutt, 2006, p. 19).

As we review or conduct our own research, we should be concerned with its validity and whether or not we can trust the findings and conclusions of the study. This is typically why we question the results of Internet and magazine articles. Although the subject of their article may be interesting, the authors usually have not utilized good research methods to arrive at their conclusions. However, their goals for writing are different than the researcher's. Often their goals are to entertain or communicate their opinion on the matter. On the other hand, the researcher's goal is to create or expand the knowledge of a specific phenomenon.

Quantitative Research Design

In order to expand or create knowledge, researchers ask important questions about the natural or social world. As discussed earlier, the research design is dependent on several factors but is primarily guided by the research question. In this section we will discuss the basic design of and concepts related to a quantitative study. Again, our research question primarily guides our design and choice of methods. For sake of this discussion let us use the following research question: Is the divorce rate among people in helping and care-giving professions higher than the general population?

Our review of the literature will help us locate the important concepts related to our research question. It is important that we **conceptualize** or specify what we mean by a specific term. For example, we will want to define helping and care-giving professions. We might define these professions as police, firefighters, doctors, nurses, clergy, and counselors. Can you think of others that should be in that list? It is also important that we **operationalize** or connect concepts to observations in our research. What could we operationalize about these types of professions? They work long hours. Their work is often stressful. For some of them their work is dangerous. What else do we know about these sub-groups of the population? The literature review will help us know more. It may also help us refine our research question. Perhaps we find out that someone has already completed a project on this topic. Does that mean we should not complete our project? Not necessarily. Perhaps the findings of the research do not seem to make sense, or perhaps we disagree with the findings. Perhaps we want to see if we can replicate the findings of the previous research. Once we make a decision about completing the research, we need at least one hypothesis to test.

A **hypothesis** is a testable prediction. Let us assume our literature review located other studies similar to our example research question so we need to refine our research question and want to know whether first responders have a higher divorce rate than the general public. First responders are conceptualized as police, firefighters, and paramedics. To formulate our hypothesis we can rephrase our question into a testable prediction. Our hypothesis in this study might be first responders have a higher divorce rate than the general public. We now have a testable prediction. We also know through our literature review that the divorce rate for the general public is roughly 40%. So we will need to construct a study that helps us determine if the divorce rate among first responders is higher than 40%.

One of the first things we need to do in designing our study is determine the **target population**, those we want to generalize our research to. Our revised research questions help us determine our target population is first responders. In order to generalize the findings of our research, we will need to sample this target population. A **sample** is a subset of our target population. We might assume that first responders who work in populations over 500,000 have similar experiences in regards to stress, work hours, danger, etc. So our survey of the sample should be targeted to first responders who work in cities with large populations. The next step in our project is to develop the actual survey instrument. We have a very simple research question, one that might be answered using secondary data. **Secondary data** is data that has already been collected by another researcher or group. For example, the U.S. Census data would be considered secondary data if you were to use it to answer a research question. We might be able to put together a data set, which is a set of information that is useful to our project and will allow us to test the hypothesis using secondary data. But for this exercise, let us construct our own instrument.

We have decided that we will construct a survey and send it out to our list of first responders. We are testing one hypothesis, that first responders do have a higher divorce rate than the general public. Let us say we find out that they do have a higher divorce rate, the next somewhat obvious question would be why do they have a higher divorce rate? We know from our literature review that they experience long work hours, high stress, and dangerous situations. Perhaps these three operationalizations would help us understand more about why they have a higher divorce rate. So why not construct a survey instrument that allows us to collect enough data to answer both of our research questions? What questions would you design? What questions do you think would help you get the answers you are looking for? I might ask questions like:

1. Have you ever been married? (If the participant answered no on this question, I could exclude them from the study because they could have never been divorced if they have never been married)
2. How many times have you been married?
3. Have you ever been divorced?
4. How many times have you been divorced?

These questions are probably enough to help us answer our first research question and test our hypothesis. We have revised our study to collect more data to answer an additional question. Why? We need more questions to help us uncover why first responders might have a higher divorce rate than the general population. Use the concepts and operationalizations and the space below to construct some of your own survey questions.

As we design our survey instrument, remember we are looking for validity. Are we creating an instrument that will allow us to see the truth? We need also be concerned with the reliability of our instrument. **Reliability** is when a test measurement produces the same results when the phenomenon does not change. If we are able to use our survey instrument among police, firefighters, paramedics, clergy, and other helping professions, and the results are consistent, our instrument is considered reliable. Now it is time to get our survey into the hands of first responders in large cities and wait for the data to come in. This is a very exciting part of research; knowing you created an instrument that might answer an important research question and seeing people respond to it. Even more exciting is considering the potential implications of your findings. What will you do with the data you gather? Finding that first responders do have a higher divorce rate and several reasons for that, what will you do? Will you publish your findings and hope someone will do something with it? You should publish your findings, but what about being more proactive with them? Perhaps you could share your findings with local first responders and work together to consider ways to increase their satisfaction with marriage. You might consider starting a program that helps first responder couples deal with specific marriage issues. We will discuss more about programs and evaluation research in another section.

Experiments

Another type of research you might come across or conduct is experimental. This type of research is often conducted in a lab with specified procedures, a test group, and a control group. The **test group** is comprised of the participants who receive the experimental treatment. The **control group** is comprised of the participants who do not receive the experimental treatment condition. The control group is typically randomly selected from the larger group of participants. Although the control group does not receive the treatment, they are still very important to the experiment. After the experiment is completed, they will be compared to the test group to find any differences in treatment results.

Experimental research is often conducted in medical research and behavioral research. In medical research we often see experiments taking place with new medicine or treatment procedures for certain diseases. For example, when a new medicine treating depression has been developed, researchers must test the medication on participants to determine its safety, side effects, and whether it works or not. These researchers would ask people to participate in the study. They would be looking specifically for people who have been diagnosed with depression and either about to be prescribed a medication or are already taking a medication that has been unsuccessful in treatment. Once the researchers have a good-sized sample in which to generalize their results to, they will randomly select the control group. The test group will receive the treatment medication and the control group will receive a placebo. Sometimes there are those in the control group who will experience the **placebo effect** where they will see improvement based on their expectations rather than the actual treatment. Once the trial is over, researchers collect data from the participants. They compare the results of the test group and the control group to determine the effectiveness of the treatment.

Harlow's Monkeys

Harry Harlow was a psychologist interested in the factors influencing the development of child attachment to their mothers. He used rhesus monkeys in his experiment. His research questions centered on whether food or security was more psychologically important for attachment to a mother. Here is a link to a video that helps explain more about Harlow's experiment, http://www.youtube.com/watch?v=hsA5Sec6dAI.

Fotokon/Shutterstock, Inc.

Behavioral scientists also conduct experiments. One such interesting experiment is Harlow's experiment on attachment in monkeys (see the spotlight on Harlow's Monkeys).

Qualitative Methods

As described above, qualitative research designs are usually an exploratory, inductive type of research that involves studying participants or behavior in their natural environment and its purpose is typically to provide rich narrative descriptions of individuals, groups, or phenomena. Previously discussed was the term generalizability. Qualitative research is not generalizable to a population or group of people, as is quantitative research. Rather it is generalizable to a specific culture (ethnography), or phenomenon (phenomenology), or process (grounded theory). One example of a great qualitative ethnographer is Dr. Jane Goodall. She is most well known for her qualitative study of the world of wild chimpanzees. She immersed herself in their world, studied their behavior, and provided the general public with a rich description of a previously little known world.

In this section we will briefly discuss three primary qualitative methods of research, phenomenology, ethnography, and grounded theory. **Phenomenology** was developed by Edmund Husserl (1859–1938). There are four major approaches to phenomenology. The first, **transcendental phenomenology** "explores the way knowledge comes into being and knowledge is based on insights rather than objective characteristics which constitutes meaning" (Richards & Morse, 2007, p. 48). The second, **existential phenomenology,** describes subjective human experience as it reflects people's values, purposes, ideals, intentions, emotions, and relationships. It is concerned with the experiences and actions of the individual, rather than conformity or behavior (Thorpe & Holt, 2007). **Hermeneutical phenomenology** is a belief that "knowledge comes into being through language and understanding" (Richards & Morse, 2007 p. 49). **Linguistical phenomenology** is the belief that language and discourse reveal the relationship between understanding, history, culture, identify, and human life (p. 49). There are two major assumptions that guide phenomenology; perceptions provide us with evidence of the world as it is lived and that human existence is meaningful. The phenomenological approach is used to study the meaning of the lived experience in a particular phenomenon. The research is concerned with understanding the essence of how people operate in the world.

Ethnography is a method that allows one to explore a particular phenomenon within culture groups. Ethnographers may be people who are part of a particular cultural group and may find it difficult to cull out specific and important values, beliefs, and behaviors of the group because of their insider stance. Ethnographers may also take an outsider stance or etic perspective where they are not part of the cultural group. Dr. Goodall would have been an outsider to the group of chimpanzees she was studying. Whether the ethnographer takes an insider or outsider stance, they are integrated as much as possible into the culture they are studying. Richards and Morse (2007) wrote of ethnography, "researchers develop thick description by processing interviews and field notes in which informal conversations and observations are reported and through theoretical insights developed from these materials" (p. 174).

Grounded theory developed by Glaser and Strauss (1967) is an approach to research that seeks to "learn from the participants [and] to understand a process or situation" (Richards & Morse, 2007, p. 60). Richards and Morse (2007) indicated that the researcher should have the perspective that change is constant and negotiable in regards to the phenomenon being studied, therefore active inquiry with "an emphasis on detailed knowledge, constant comparison, and the trajectory of the event" (p. 61), is vital to the research. One goal when using a grounded theory approach is to achieve saturation with the data and is achieved "when categories are well defined and no new variation [is] discovered" (Weaver, Wuest, & Ciliska, 2005). The main strategies for analyzing data in grounded theory are comparative. Transcriptions of interviews might be open coded, memoed, categorized, and integrated. The researcher might make notes during interviews and memos afterward; the entirety of this information would then be used to construct a theory of the phenomenon being studied. During the analysis, a timeline of events might be constructed using the information from interviews. Constructing a timeline might be beneficial in comparing participants' experiences in an effort to uncover a process that is similar for all who experience the same phenomenon. The analysis of the transcribed interviews is meant to provide new insight or understanding into the process and experience of the phenomenon.

Evaluation Research

In the previous section on quantitative research we briefly introduced the idea of program evaluation as a type of research. This type of research usually occurs when a **stakeholder**, someone who has a vested interest in a program, wants to know whether a program is successful. Previously, we considered starting a marriage program for first responders based on the data we uncovered in our research. We will not discuss the development of a program here but it is important to consider how you will know your program is successful or not. What will the goals of the program be? What do you hope to achieve? Perhaps a lower divorce rate among first responders, but perhaps a more likely goal would be a healthy satisfaction with their marriage relationship. It is easier to plan for evaluation at the outset than to evaluate the success of a poorly planned program. However, a poorly planned program can still be evaluated. You may come across this kind of research among helping professions, not for profit organizations, and non-governmental organizations (NGOs).

Reporting Research

The way one reports their research is dependent on the type of research conducted. In this chapter we have discussed quantitative, qualitative, mixed method, and case study approaches. We have also discussed evaluation research. In addition to those types of research, we should briefly mention that an exhaustive literature review can also be an approach to research. This is more commonly referred to as a **meta-analysis,** a quantitative research method where published research studies of the same research question are treated as cases and then analyzed for patterns in the findings.

Many researchers report their findings in academic research journals. Writing for academic journals is thought to be some of the hardest writing because it is reviewed by other experts in the same field before it can be considered for publication. Reputable academic journals usually have a very low acceptance rate, between 10 and 20%, and many times even these reports are accepted only after making required revisions to their report based on the reviewer's comments. The audience for these reports is generally other researchers who may or may not be academicians. In recent years there has been a push for academic journals that are more lenient on publication standards. These types of journals are referred to as open journals. Open journals are still academic in nature, but the requirements to publish in them are different than the standard academic journals. Some open journals are peer-reviewed similar to standard journals but many are not. The primary argument against open journals is centered on the "pay to publish" idea. Essentially anyone who has completed a research report could pay the publisher of the journal to publish in an open journal where it may not have been reviewed by other experts in the field. These payments are usually outrageous and range from several hundred dollars to sometimes over a thousand dollars. While open journals may eventually find their place in academia they are generally not thought of as reputable among academicians. Researchers may also publish a research report that is meant for a more general audience or perhaps a report for a funding agency or organization. No matter which one of these reports you might read or write, they will be structured and have the same basic information within them. Both types of report will have an introduction of the problem and review of the important literature of the topic or field. The report will then generally discuss the research question, hypotheses, and design of the study. Afterward, the report will describe the results or the findings of the study. Finally, the report will provide a discussion or interpretation of the findings. Some researchers may also desire to have their findings reported to an even more general audience. They may discuss their findings and interpretations of their research in trade publications, organizational newsletters, and books.

Ethics

When conducting research it is important to consider the ethical nature of what you want to accomplish. Perhaps you have an important research question, but the design of your study has the potential to harm the participants in your sample in some way. It is important to consider your sample whether they are participating in a simple quantitative survey, a qualitative interview, or experimental treatment. Is there a possibility that they may be harmed physically, psychologically, emotionally, or in some other way? Are there any long-term negative effects associated with participating in your research? Is participating in your research study confidential? These questions involve the safety of **human subjects,** or living individuals. There are also ethical considerations for having animals participate in your research study. Scientists who conduct research have not always considered the ethical implications of their research. One of the most famous studies often cited when discussing ethical considerations is the Stanford Prison Experiment. Find out more about it in the feature below.

Institutional review boards (IRB) are charged with reviewing plans for research and ensuring the protection of human subjects. The IRB has developed over time as a result of experiments like the one described above. One of the earliest and often-cited examples of research abuse in the United States is the study of syphilis in Tuskegee, Alabama. Young, poor, black men were purposefully infected with the syphilis disease and not informed. Years later when these men found out they had the disease, they were refused treatment. If you are to conduct any reputable research, your project plan must be submitted to an IRB for review. Their job is to ensure your planned research is ethical and would not cause any harm to your human subjects.

Stanford Prison Experiment

In the summer of 1971, researchers led by psychologist Philip Zimbardo at Stanford University conducted an experiment on the psychology of prison life. Students who participated in the experiment were randomly assigned the role of a guard or prisoner. After only a short time, the students assigned to the role of guard began to abuse the prisoners psychologically and physically. The researchers allowed the abuse to go on. Two of the student prisoners quit the experiment early, and the entire experiment was abruptly stopped after six days. Part of the experiment was filmed and excerpts are publicly available. Here is a link to a documentary of the experiment filmed at a later time, http://www.youtube.com/watch?v=1Py3JJZ2ZrI.

f8grapher/Shutterstock, Inc.

References

Christensen, L. B., Johnson, B., & Turner, L. A. (2011). *Research methods, design, and analysis*. Boston: Allyn & Bacon.

Cronbach, L. J. (1971). Test validation. In R. L. Thorndike (Ed.), *Educational Measurement* (2nd ed., pp. 443–507). Washington, DC: American Council on Education.

Glaser, B. G., & Strauss, A. L. (1967). *The discovery of grounded theory: Strategies for qualitative research*. Chicago: Aldine.

Myers, M. (2000). Qualitative research and the generalizability question: Standing firm with Proteus. *The Qualitative Report, 4*(3/4), 1–9.

Richards, L., & Morse, J. M. (2007). *Read me first for a user's guide to qualitative methods* (2nd ed.). Thousand Oaks, CA: Sage.

Schutt, R. K. (2006). *Investigating the social world: The process and practice of research* (5th ed.) Newbury Park, CA: Pine Forge Press.

Thorpe, R., & Holt, R. (2007). *The Sage dictionary of qualitative management research*. Thousand Oaks, CA: Sage.

Trumbull, M. (2005). Qualitative research methods. In G. R. Taylor (Ed.), *Integrating qualitative and qualitative methods in research* (pp. 101–124). Lanham, MD: University Press of America.

Venkatesh, V., Brown, S. A., & Bala, H. (2013). Bridging the qualitative-quantitative divide: Guidelines for conducting mixed methods research in information systems. *Mis Quarterly, 37*(1), 21–54.

Weaver, K., Wuest, J., & Ciliska, D. (2005). Understanding women's journey of recovering from anorexia nervosa. *Qual Health Res, 15*(2), 188–206. doi:10.1177/1049732304270819

Yin, R. K. (1994). *Case study research: Design and methods*. Thousand Oaks: Sage

CHAPTER 7

Introduction to Interdisciplinary Research

Understanding the basics of research methods is important as we begin to move into the process of interdisciplinary research. While disciplinary research has been very successful and provided a wealth of knowledge, Repko, Szostak, and Buchberger (2013) conclude it "suffers from several defects that limit its ability to address a whole new class of problems that confront nature and human society" (p. 199). Thus an interdisciplinary research process is better suited to address the complex problems of our world. **Interdisciplinary research** "is to study a topic or question that is inherently complex and whose parts are the focus of two or more disciplines, integrate their insights, and construct a more comprehensive understanding of the topic or question" (p. 199). As we begin to discuss the interdisciplinary research process specifically, you need to be aware of the problems associated with attempting interdisciplinary research. Attempting this process is not easy, especially when one is working with disciplinary perspectives they are not trained in. Trying to find connections between disciplines can often be difficult. Working in teams, which is how much of interdisciplinary research is often completed, adds difficulty and complexity to the interdisciplinary research process (IRP). Working with people that have different views, beliefs, and personalities can be challenging. Sometimes the problem or issue under investigation is not complex enough to need an interdisciplinary perspective.

Conditions for Successful Interdisciplinary Research

Petrie (1976) discusses conditions necessary in order for interdisciplinary research to be successful. First, the project must have **idea dominance** which is defined as "a clear and recognizable idea which can serve as a central focus for the work" (p. 32). As one engages in interdisciplinary research, whether tackled as an individual or through a small group, there are important questions to ask. What is the problem or research question(s)? Is the problem clear? Does everyone involved in the research group understand the problem? Is this idea or problem complex enough to require interdisciplinarity? Second, successful interdisciplinary projects include a **need for achievement**. In other words, there must be a purpose behind the interdisciplinary project. The project needs a clear pathway towards success. Especially when working in research groups, those involved in the project need to have a sense that the project can be successful. The idea/concept/research problem must keep the interest of those involved. No matter how interesting a project is, if it fails to produce results people will eventually give up on it. **Peer recognition** is also necessary for successful interdisciplinary research. There are two ways that peer recognition is important. First as it relates to your academic program; students want to know that their degree is meaningful and that their academic experience can be useful to their career and future plans. Second, as it relates to interdisciplinary research, engage in meaningful interdisciplinary research; something that has intrinsic and extrinsic value. Interdisciplinary research should have an application to and for other people, society at large, or a local community. Finally, certain **psychological traits** or characteristics that almost all interdisciplinarians share are needed. We will discuss more about interdisciplinary characteristics in a later chapter.

Assuming you have the conditions necessary to engage in interdisciplinary research, you need to have a complex problem or project that requires an interdisciplinary perspective before moving on. We have already discussed several processes to interdisciplinary research (e.g., Repko's 10 steps, Klein's 11 steps, and Newell's 12 steps). For sake of parsimony, we will discuss an interdisciplinary research process using five steps. The first step of which is to define the problem or state the research question. It is the first and most basic step in conducting any kind of research, whether it is interdisciplinary or disciplinary. So here is an example: How do we bring down and stabilize the cost of gas? That is a research question. But, is this research question complex enough to require an interdisciplinary perspective? As mentioned in an earlier chapter, Newell (2001) discussed the often systemic nature of questions that are complex enough to require an interdisciplinary approach to research. Thus the second step for interdisciplinary students is to understand the complexity of a particular question or problem before engaging in interdisciplinary research. As you write for assignments, publication, or projects, it is important that you justify your interdisciplinary approach. Answering questions like: Why is this problem complex? What perspectives are important in helping us understand more about this problem? and other meaningful questions you could ask about a particular question or problem. Ensure that your stated question or problem is complex and that insights from at least two disciplinary perspectives are available. Suppose we continue on in this interdisciplinary research process on bringing down and stabilizing the cost of gas; it would require us to know something about the gas and oil industry, right? Those are two related, but different, industries. It would require us to know something about the government's involvement in the regulation of these industries, which is a completely separate disciplinary perspective.

The third step in this process is to locate multiple sources of disciplinary knowledge that relate to the subject of study. Repko (2012) discusses this task as identifying potentially relevant disciplines. As one identifies potentially relevant disciplines the goal is to narrow down that list to the most relevant disciplines. Again, we are discussing this in the context of our gasoline problem. Students often make the mistake of listing too many disciplines or disciplines that have no relevance to a particular problem. In my view, the research question or problem informs our list of most relevant disciplines and makes listing potentially relevant disciplines unnecessary.

One might argue that a research question may not be informative enough to provide a quick list of most relevant disciplines. I would then argue that the research question is not clear enough thus could not be studied. Again, Repko (2012) posits that in order to move on in an interdisciplinary research process, the researcher(s) must develop adequacy in the epistemology of the most relevant disciplines. In our example, we need to locate information that would help us understand more about the oil and gas industry. We assume that the most relevant disciplines or perspectives might be petroleum engineering, public policy, and economics. If one has not studied any of these disciplines moving on in the process can be difficult. However, there is Repko's argument that one need not be an expert in any given discipline; rather, they should become adequate in the disciplinary epistemology. **Adequacy** is defined as "an understanding of each discipline's cognitive map sufficient to identify its perspective, epistemology, assumptions, concepts, theories, and methods in order to understand its insights into a particular problem" (Repko, 2012, p. 60).

In order to become adequate in a discipline one needs to review salient literature to the discipline and subject. As one reads through the literature, they might discover that a particular discipline does not provide any insight into the research problem. If so, the research must ask again if the question requires an interdisciplinary perspective and what other disciplines might be most relevant. As one continues to review the literature, they should begin to understand more about the disciplinary insights related to the research question. Another tool that will be useful in this step is a **cognitive map**. Creating a cognitive map will help you develop some adequacy of the disciplinary epistemologies that you are using in an IDS research project. For those conducting interdisciplinary research, the cognitive map of disciplinary perspective is important. Cognitive maps help us understand the elements of a discipline; its basic concepts, theories, research methods, and standards of proof (Petrie, 1976).

As we consider the epistemology of disciplinary perspectives, we need also to consider their world views and assumptions. We should consider leading theories and thinkers of our interdisciplinary problem. It may also be of importance to consider who the leading practitioners are and the work they have already accomplished in a particular area related to our interdisciplinary project. Asking ourselves the following questions may also be helpful as we search out information related to our interdisciplinary project. What has already been written about a particular complex problem or issue? Who are the authors that have already written about it? Who are the researchers that have already researched the problem? What are the leading academic journals that are publishing research articles on a particular problem or issue? Are there any professional associations that are associated with a particular discipline that is studying a complex problem or issue? In addition, you are looking to discover relevant disciplinary insights into your research problem. What do the disciplines have to say about your interdisciplinary problem? What have researchers already discovered about your problem? Essentially, in this step, you are trying to discover as much information as you can about the interdisciplinary problem from each disciplinary perspective. After completing this step, you would have an adequate understanding of how petroleum is engineered into gasoline, and an adequate understanding of how regulatory policies are created as well as how specific polices affect the oil and gas industry. You would also want to know how gas prices affect the consumer and to a larger degree the economy.

The fourth step in this process is to identify conflicts and connections between the disciplinary insights above. We previously discussed the notion that identifying conflicts and connections required us to "unpack disciplinary boxes." As we identify the conflicts and connection between the disciplinary perspectives, the goal is to find common ground. Repko (2012) defines **common ground** as "that which is created between conflicting disciplinary insights or theories, preparatory for performing integration and producing an interdisciplinary product" (pp. 56–57). The concept of integration is required for interdisciplinary research. If there is no integration of disciplinary insights then the work is multidisciplinary rather than interdisciplinary.

The final step in this process is to construct a more comprehensive understanding of the problem or issue. This comprehensive understanding is the integrative framework that helps people understand a problem from a holistic perspective rather than a disciplinary perspective. Repko (2012) explains that one must have a **common ground integrator**, "the one or more assumptions, concepts, or theoretical explanations by which conflicting insights can be integrated" (pp 267–268) in order to help develop or create an integrative framework for understanding the interdisciplinary problem.

Conditions for Integration

There are three conditions for performing integration. First, you have to overcome disciplinarity. Overcoming disciplinarity involves the ability to view a problem from multiple perspectives rather than one disciplinary perspective. For example, if a researcher is trained in biology and wants to study a complex problem the researcher needs to have the ability to consider the problem from a biological perspective without rejecting other disciplinary insights. Repko (2012) discusses three cognitive abilities one needs in order to overcome disciplinarity; perspective taking, balancing different disciplinary views, and holistic thinking. **Perspective taking** is "viewing some problem, object, or phenomenon from a standpoint other than one's own" (p. 274). As we discussed in Chapter 5, Leonard (2012) saw this as a necessary ability for her students' successful integrative learning. Our perspective or worldview is shaped by our values, beliefs, and learning. Often we become strong willed in our perspective of the world refusing to see that there may be other explanations. Interdisciplinarians must have the ability to see problems from perspectives other than their own. **Balancing conflicting viewpoints** is also a necessary skill for interdisciplinarians and requires that they consider disciplinary insights that provide conflicting information about a complex problem. It is a process of sorting the strengths and weaknesses of disciplinary insights. It is a "crucial step toward integrating ideas" (Repko, 2012, p. 277). **Holistic thinking** is also a necessary cognitive ability. It is the ability to understand how disciplinary insights relate to each other and to the problem (Repko, 2012).

The second condition required for integration is to triangulate depth, breath, and integration or **interdisciplinary triangulation** (Figure 7.1).

FIGURE 7.1

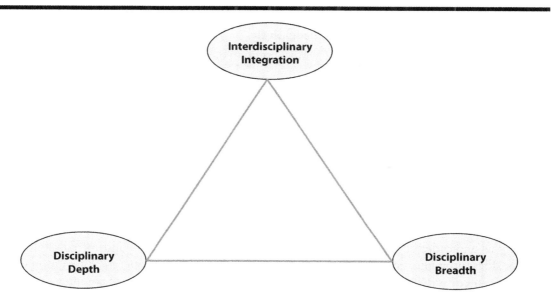

Klein (1996) and Repko (2012) discuss the need for interdisciplinarians to have a **disciplinary depth** referring to disciplinary knowledge. Repko also calls this being adequate in a discipline. **Disciplinary breadth** refers to the knowledge that has been produced by disciplines, sub-disciplines, interdisciplines, and experts concerning a specific problem. **Interdisciplinary integration** then is the culmination of the process of developing a new holistic understanding of a complex problem. However, Klein (2015) discusses a newer concept of quadrangulating disciplinary depth, **multidisciplinary breadth**, multidisciplinary and **transdisciplinary integration**, and **interprofessional cooperation**. Klein expands her original idea by adding that interdisciplinary students are exposed to multiple disciplines as a cornerstone of their education, and therefore it is necessary that they know how to find relevant knowledge and information and integrate in order to widen the scope of study. Both interdisciplinarity and transdisciplinarity "couple depth and breadth in a process of weighing multiple perspectives and generating a synthesis or more holistic understanding" (p. 12). She further discusses four skills needed to foster broad-based reflective learning; cognitive flexibility, communicating collaboratively, leveraging integration, and navigating knowledge and information critically.

Finally, Repko (2012) discusses the third condition necessary for integration in interdisciplinary research, cultivating the seven qualities of mind:

1. seeking what is useful even if it is problematic,
2. thinking inclusively and integratively,
3. not exclusively, being responsive to each perspective but dominated by none,

4. striving for balance among conflicting disciplinary perspectives and insights,

5. maintaining intellectual flexibility,

6. thinking both inductively end deductively,

7. and thinking about the whole while simultaneously working with parts.

These qualities of mind are characteristic of skills and traits of interdisciplinarians that we will discuss further in a later chapter.

Moving Beyond Interdisciplinarity

Klein's (2015) discussion on quadrangulation is what helps us move beyond interdisciplinarity into integrative learning. Repko's (2012) interdisciplinary research process provides a helpful and informative model for conducting interdisciplinary research. He discusses the notion of integration as being the critical ingredient for interdisciplinarity. However, integration and integrative learning as an academic movement provide opportunities to think beyond interdisciplinarity and consider the application of such to the world in which we live and operate. Integration in the context of interdisciplinary research creates a new holistic understanding of complex problems. Integration in the context of lived experiences creates a new holistic understanding and application of interdisciplinarity. Integration, as interdisciplinary scholars would agree, means to synthesize. Interdisciplinary scholars create new meaning, but without synthesizing or integrating with life, what good is it? Whether in the context of life or learning, the concept(s) of integration challenge us to think about ways to connect and apply knowledge and information from one area of our life to other areas of our life.

Mapping the Problem

In the previous section we discussed identifying potentially relevant disciplines that might inform our complex problem. In this section, we will briefly discuss the concept of **mapping the problem**. You will need to, as clearly as possible, understand the complex problem you are trying to research. Part of the process of understanding the problem means that you will need to have a clearly defined interdisciplinary research question or problem. As mentioned earlier, the research question or problem helps us identify the potentially relevant disciplines. As we learn more about the problem we may discover that our initial list of potentially relevant disciplines will not provide us with the necessary insight(s) to create a new holistic understanding. We discussed previously that a review of the salient literature was an effective way to uncover relevant disciplinary insight, information, or knowledge that informs our complex problem. We also discussed the concept of cognitive maps. Here we discuss categorizing cognitive processing maps into three types of maps that will help us frame our interdisciplinary research. These types of cognitive processing maps are the **research map**, the **concept or principle map**, and the **theory map** (Repko, 2012). Each one of these maps may be helpful in framing your interdisciplinary research.

In our five step process discussed above, we have a complex problem to research. Our research question informs or guides us towards the potentially relevant disciplines that may provide information about our problem. We may want to conduct a preliminary or cursory check of the disciplinary literature to decide whether our list of potentially relevant disciplines may in fact be informative. We want to know whether there are published, scholarly articles on any aspect of the problem. In selecting disciplines from which to draw disciplinary insights, our goal is to decide which disciplines contribute substantially to the problem. This will help us narrow down the list of potentially relevant disciplines to the most relevant disciplines. In doing so, you should consider which disciplines might consider the phenomena relevant for study. Make a long list of any discipline you think may be able to provide insight into the research problem. As you make this list ask yourself "Does it shed light on the some aspect of the problem?" Have experts in a discipline published research on the problem? There is no need to conduct a full literature review at this point. You simply want to locate information that may be relevant to the problem you are studying. Using an online database at the school's library (e.g., EBSCO) or an online search engine like www.google.com/scholar would be good for this exercise. Briefly read through some of the literature. Confirm whether it has any bearing on the research problem. As you are searching for and reading through potentially relevant disciplinary literature, making annotations of the sources would be helpful. An **annotated bibliography** of each key source includes the following pieces of information; the full citation of the source, and a summary of the article or source (two or three sentences). You may find it helpful to also include the following items in an annotated bibliography: your evaluation, in three or four sentences, of the ideas presented in the article or source and a log of articles or sources you found but may not have actually read.

After you have narrowed down your potentially relevant disciplines to the most relevant disciplines, creating a map of each one may be of help to you. We will briefly discuss each one. First, create a research map of each discipline in your list of most relevant disciplines. The research map will state the purpose of the research, the perspectives of each discipline concerning the problem, the assumptions of each discipline, and identifies non-disciplinary sources or interpretations. Second, you may want to create a concept or principle map that breaks down the problem into its constituent parts and helps you locate or identify related disciplinary insights. As you work on this type of mapping, anticipate how each part of the problem may relate to the whole. Look for meaningful relationship between the parts of the problem. You may want to ask yourself the following questions:

- ▶ What is the name of the concept or principle?
- ▶ What is a good description of the concept or principle?
- ▶ Why is the concept or principle important?
- ▶ What theories are related to this concept or principle?
- ▶ Are there any related concepts or principles?
- ▶ What research has been conducted?

Finally, creating a theory map will help you describe theories that provide supporting evidence, importance related to your research question. You may want to ask yourself the following questions:

- ► What is a good description of the theory?
- ► What evidence is there for and against this theory?
- ► Why is the theory important?
- ► Are there any similar or analogous theories?
- ► Which theories compete with this one?

During the creation of your cognitive maps, you will be conducting the literature review. We have already discussed the purposes of the basic literature review and how the literature review helps us develop adequacy in the relevant disciplines. It also helps us in the following ways:

- ► To save time and effort
- ► To discover what scholarly knowledge has been produced on the topic by different discipline
- ► To narrow the topic and sharpen the focus of the research question
- ► To identify the factors that have contributed to the development of the problem over time
- ► To reveal the paths of prior disciplinary research and how the proposed interdisciplinary project is linked to these and may extend them
- ► To situate or contextualize the problem
- ► To identify the defining elements used by each discipline's experts in their writing on the problem
- ► To verify that disciplinary insights are relevant

Although we have discussed a number of challenges, confronting interdisciplinarians doing interdisciplinary research presents even more. There is more information to be covered. We must review relevant literature from multiple disciplines as opposed to one. Interdisciplinary researchers risk being seduced by what disciplinary experts say (Repko, 2012). In other words, we may be overcome by the evidence that one discipline presents concerning a particular topic, so much so that we give up on our research agenda. Interdisciplinarians must place the insights and theories of each relevant discipline within the context of its unique perspective. Interdisciplinarians create new knowledge or understanding by synthesizing multiple knowledges of a given problem or issue. Finally, the methods of library and database cataloguing disadvantage interdisciplinary researchers.

References

Klein, J. T. (2015). Beyond Interdisciplinarity: Expanding Horizons of Integrative Learning. In P. C. Hughes, J. S. Munoz, & M. N. Tanner (Eds.), *Perspectives in Interdisciplinary and Integrative Studies* (Vol. 1). Lubbock, TX: Texas Tech University Press.

Leonard, J. B. (2012). Integrative learning: A grounded theory. *Issues in Integrative Studies* (30), 48–74.

Newell, W. H. (2001). A theory of interdisciplinary studies. *Issues in Integrative Studies, 19*, 1–25.

Petrie, H. G. (1976). Do you see what I see? The epistemology of interdisciplinary inquiry. *Journal of Aesthetic Education*, 29–43.

Repko, A. F. (2012). *Interdisciplinary research: Process and theory* (2nd ed.). Thousand Oaks, CA: Sage.

Repko, A. F., Szostak, R. R., & Buchberger, M. P. (2013). *Introduction to interdisciplinary studies.* Thousand Oaks, CA: Sage.

CHAPTER 8

Methods of Integration

In this chapter, we will discuss the last two steps of interdisciplinary research, synthesizing and creating a new integrative framework for understanding a complex problem. Dewey (1910) said, "The essence of critical thinking is suspended judgment; and the essence of this suspense is inquiry to determine the nature of the problem before proceeding to attempts at its solution" (p. 74). Much of what we learned in the first three steps allows us to suspend our judgment in the interest of inquiry about the complex problem. As part of the fourth step then, interdisciplinary researchers are looking for conflicts, connections, patterns, and discontinuities between disciplinary insights pertaining to the problem being studied. As you engage in this part of the interdisciplinary research process you should be critically thinking and evaluating disciplinary insights as a way to create common ground. As discussed previously, creating common ground between disciplinary insights helps us to synthesize or integrate those insights as a way to move to step five. In step five then, we are creating a new integrative or holistic understanding of the complex problem.

Knowledge transfer is one way to think about interdisciplinary integration and moving towards a new holistic framework of understanding. Knowledge transfer is the ability to utilize learning from one context in a new context (Perkins & Salomon, 1988). Perkins and Salomon (1992a) define the transfer of learning as

> Transfer of learning occurs when learning in one context or with one set of materials impacts on performance in another context or with other related materials. For example, learning to drive a car helps a person later to learn more quickly to drive a truck, learning mathematics prepares students to study physics, learning to get along with one's siblings may prepare one for getting along better with others, and experience playing chess might even make one a better strategic thinker in politics or business. (p. 1)

The knowledge you gain by working through the first three steps should transfer or "travel" through the filter of step number four and finally arrive in a new context in step number five. In addition, the pragmatic or sensible knowledge you have about research or a complex problem in general should inform your work in these last two steps. In this chapter, we will discuss two types of knowledge or learning transfer, **near** and **far**. We will also discuss two mechanisms for knowledge transfer, **low road transfer** and **high road transfer,** and three bridges for learning.

Types of Transfer

Transfer of learning infers that some "travel" between learning contexts has been made, where learning in one setting is applied to another situation, precipitating expanded and/or new understanding. The distance of travel dictates whether one of two types of transfer is involved: **near** transfer or **far** transfer. Perkins and Salomon (1992), define near transfer as "transfer between very similar contexts" (p. 3). For example, a builder who is constructing a board-on-board privacy fence may have never done so before but because he has built a standard fence, working with similar posts, stringers, tools and wood planks, he is able to engage in near transfer to construct the privacy fence. Far transfer, on the other hand, "refers to transfer between contexts that, on appearance seem remote and alien to one another" (Perkins & Salomon, 1992, p. 3). In far transfer, tasks may look completely different but are actually similar conceptually. For example, "a chess player might apply basic strategic principles such as 'take control of the center' to investment practices, politics, or military campaigns" (Perkins & Salomon, 1992b). Because there is a decrease in the degree of similarity and pragmatic relevance between knowledge contexts, far transfer presents challenges for students (Hung, 2013). "Far transfer also requires more modification of the original knowledge than near transfer to adapt to the target transfer condition" (Hung, 2013, p. 29).

Mechanisms of Transfer

Salomon and Perkins (1989) characterize the two mechanisms for learning transfer in the way that "high-road transfer involves deliberate reflective processing" and "low-road transfer depends on pattern recognition and the reflexive triggering of routines" (Perkins & Salomon, 2012, p. 251). Transfer along the low road occurs when skills are well practiced and the learner encounters a context with apparent perceptual similarities to the original domain of learning. Low road transfer is basically the transfer of knowledge from one context to another that is similar. In the case of low road transfer, it is more likely to occur since common surface features essentially cue the employment of automatized processes. For example, encountering printed text automatically cues the reader to read what is there. When low road transfer is involved, behavior is often automatic—you know what to do without having to think about it much. One example or one way that you can think about low road transfer is, once you learn how to drive a standard car you can easily transfer that knowledge to driving a van, a bus, or a semi-tractor trailer. There may be some slight variations in how you drive each one of those vehicles but the basic skills needed are the same—you get into the car, you turn the key, you use the steering wheel, perhaps there is a stick shift or maybe there's a shifting lever on the steering column, but the knowledge needed to operate the vehicle is primarily automatic. The rules of the road are primarily the same no matter where you might drive in America. Even if you were to drive a vehicle in a different country where they perhaps drive on a different side of the road, transferring your knowledge of driving in one context to another similar context is an example of low road transfer.

The second type is high road transfer, when the new learning context differs considerably from the original. The learner must call upon a higher metacognitive application of what he or she knows or knows how to do. In these cases, similarities lie far beneath the surface, requiring deliberation and reflection to identify the principles or analogical relationships that tie together the seemingly dissimilar frameworks. In high road transfer, the learner must ask questions where the answers are not automatic or obvious: "What is the general pattern in this problem, what do I need to solve it? What principles might apply here?" (Perkins & Salmon, 1992). High road transfer depends on a deliberate mindful abstraction of skill or knowledge from one context or application to another. One example of high road transfer might be applying skills and abilities in driving a vehicle to flying a plane. We might ask ourselves: how is navigation similar? how is the general operation of a plane similar to driving a car? This transfer of knowledge would require us to pull from other knowledge sources as well. I have talked a little bit about my professional experience in retail, ministry, and at the university. If I were to engage in high road transfer, I might consider a skill that I learned in retail and ask how I might be able to transfer or apply similar principles to what I am doing in my work at the university.

There are many skills that I have learned in my career experiences. One skill is working with people. I learned through multiple experiences that good customer service matters. It matters to the customer, to one's supervisor, and will eventually matter to you or you will likely find a different line of work where having this skill is not important. Working in retail if I wanted to please my supervisor I would work hard to provide good customer service. Most days utilizing this skill helped me leave work feeling good that I had helped someone. Later when I transitioned into full-time pastoral ministry, those good customer service skills translated well. Every day my "job" or ministry was to help people. I had to understand them, their context, their culture, their life's experience, in a way, to be able to help them. The skill also transfers to my work at the university. I must have good customer service skills to be successful. Students are my customer. Other staff, faculty, and administrators on the campus are my customer. In order to be successful I have to be able to transfer those good customer service skills to this new context. The example I just shared is one of **backwards reaching transfer** where I must reach back in time, back in my own life's experiences, to locate examples of good and bad customer service and how the lessons I learned might apply to my current context or situation. **Forward reaching transfer** is when one learns something in abstract preparation for an application elsewhere, in a new and different context. An example of forward reaching transfer is to consider how you can utilize what you are learning now, at the university, and use it in preparation for your future. It involves reflective thought and abstracting from one context and seeking connections with other contexts. Consider how you might use concepts, skills, and abilities you learn in integrative studies courses or psychology courses or engineering courses as you prepare for your career and future.

While many students utilize low road transfer to simply get by in their education, arguably the better students utilize high road transfer to challenge and prepare themselves for a successful future. There are two other terms that are related to low road and high road transfer. **Hugging** is one way to think about low road transfer. Transfer of learning does not necessarily happen without intervention. Intervention may come in the form of a student learning and implementing concepts learned in the classroom. Students should intentionally foster the concepts of knowledge transfer. Hugging helps students to engage low road transfer mechanisms by making explicit connections between two similar, or near, contexts of desired transfer.

Bridging is another practice used to facilitate the more difficult mechanisms of high road transfer. **Bridging** is a mediated process that recognizes connections between contexts that are related only on an abstract level. The relationship between Mr. Miyagi and Daniel in the movie *Karate Kid* provides an excellent example of bridging. Mr. Miyagi assigns chores to Daniel as a way to transfer certain abilities to karate so that he might block vertically (painting) and horizontally (car waxing). Miyagi calls attention to these learned skills from disparate domains and, in so doing, achieves successful far or high road transfer.

Bridges for Transfer of Learning

Perkins and Salomon (2012) discuss three bridges for transfer of learning; detect, elect, and connect. They view these bridges "as functions to be fulfilled one way or another on any occasion of transfer" (p. 250). **Detecting** "means discerning the possibility of a connection" (p. 253). As we engage in earlier steps of the interdisciplinary research process, we should be detecting the possibilities of connections we might make in later steps. **Connecting** "addresses the challenge of finding a relevant relationship between initial learning and the transfer situation" (p. 252). We have already discussed how important it is to find the connections between disciplinary insights as it relates to a complex problem under study. **Elect** "means choosing to pursue a possible connection" (p. 255). As we prepare to move to step five, we need to decide what connections are the most important. We must choose the pathways or connections that will help us create a more holistic understanding of the complex problem.

Interdisciplinary Integration

We have discussed the concept of interdisciplinary integration in the previous chapter. Integration in the context of interdisciplinary studies research means simply to synthesize. Klein (1990) discusses interdisciplinary integration as being the litmus test of interdisciplinarity, meaning if there is no integration, it is not interdisciplinary. Think about integrate as a verb, meaning to unite or blend into a functioning whole. It is the interdisciplinary integration that helps you to create a new holistic understanding; a new framework for understanding a complex problem. Interdisciplinary integration is a gradual process which culminates in a new, more comprehensive understanding. Repko (2012) describes this new holistic understanding as the product or the result of the integrative process.

References

Dewey, J. (1910). *How we think*. New York: Heath.

Hung, W. (2013). Problem-Based Learning: A Learning Environment for Enhancing Learning Transfer. *New Directions for Adult and Continuing Education, 2013* (137), 27–38.

Klein, J. T. (1990). *Interdisciplinarity: history, theory, & practice*. Detroit, MI: Wayne State University Press.

Perkins, D. N., & Salomon, G. (1988). Teaching for transfer. *Educational leadership, 46*(1), 22–32.

Perkins, D. N., & Salomon, G. (1992a). The science and art of transfer. *If minds matter: A foreword to the future, 1*, 201–210.

Perkins, D. N., & Salomon, G. (1992b). Transfer of learning. *International Encyclopedia of Education* (2nd ed.). Oxford, England: Pergamon Press.

Perkins, D. N., & Salomon, G. (2012). Knowledge to go: A motivational and dispositional view of transfer. *Educational Psychologist, 47*(3), 248–258.

Repko, A. F. (2012). *Interdisciplinary research: Process and theory* (2nd ed.). Thousand Oaks, CA: Sage.

Salomon, G., & Perkins, D. N. (1989). Rocky roads to transfer: Rethinking mechanism of a neglected phenomenon. *Educational Psychologist, 24*(2), 113–142.

PART III

Interdisciplinary Priorities

CHAPTER 9

Describing Interdisciplinary and Integrative Learners

As we move into part three of this textbook, you may have noticed that being an interdisciplinarian, engaging in interdisciplinary research and integrative learning, is not necessarily an easy task. You may have also considered that having the skills and abilities necessary to be an interdisciplinarian are acquired and nurtured, not necessarily an innate part of who we are. They are deliberate activities on your part. In terms of your interdisciplinary degree choice, you may have been questioning that decision. In the rest of this textbook my goal is to lead you toward understanding the advantages of interdisciplinarity and integrative learning. It is my hope that by the time you finish this textbook you will see yourself as an interdisciplinarian and integrative learner, having an understanding of how powerful an interdisciplinary degree can be for your career and future plans. Although you may have initially chosen an interdisciplinary degree because it was the fastest path to graduation, I hope you will have a greater understanding of the value of interdisciplinary and integrative studies by the time you finish engaging in the remaining part of this text. In part three, we will focus our learning on what I call priorities of interdisciplinary and integrative learning. Specifically, in Chapter 9, we will discuss advantages and disadvantages of interdisciplinary and integrative studies as well as some of the characteristics of interdisciplinarians. Chapter 10 will focus on the notions that interdisciplinary and integrative learners must be able to work in teams and utilize a global perspective when dealing with certain complex problems. Chapter 11 will round out part three by focusing on the concept of continuity and helping you construct your interdisciplinary story. In this chapter, let us first briefly discuss how metaphors can help us better understand the concepts of interdisciplinary and integrative learning.

Speaking Metaphorically

A metaphor is one word or an expression used in comparison of another thing, idea, action, to suggest some similarity or common quality between the two. Usually it compares something concrete with something abstract. An example of a metaphorical expression is "a laugh in a sea

The Mycelia Project

The Mycelia Project is an interdisciplinary educational project collaboration with Chicago Public Schools, Urban Gateways, and the Woodlawn Community Development Corporation. The goals of the experimental projects are to promote learning focused on food, soil, water, and energy sustainability. Those involved in the Mycelia Project utilized art to visually present the creative processes, which included constructing an aquaponics garden.

rangizzz/Shutterstock, Inc.

https://www.youtube.com/watch?v=1mqhHTFY0vw

of sadness." We might interpret this metaphor to mean there is hope in the impossible. There are differences between a metaphor and the simile. Interdisciplinarians typically do not use simile to describe interdisciplinarity. A simile compares two things using like or as. You probably remember learning about the differences between metaphor and simile in grade school. Some examples of simile are "as sly as a fox," "as free as a bird," and "' like two peas in a pod."

Types of Metaphors

There are different types of metaphors that you should be aware of, especially as it relates to interdisciplinary and integrative learning. There are dead metaphors, mixed metaphors, and interdisciplinary metaphors. **Dead metaphors** are those that have become clichés or have lost effectiveness through frequent use (e.g., "all walks of life"). **Mixed metaphors** are the result of applying two metaphors to one thing resulting in a confusing or illogical comparison. Because metaphors are a linguistic tool to help us make our point more vivid, mixing metaphors leads to confusion. One example might be "wake up and smell the coffee on the wall." Another might be "I'm sweating bullets." There are also **interdisciplinary metaphors,** which are metaphors that help people who are unfamiliar with this concept better understand it. There are a number of metaphors that have already been utilized that bring to life the concepts related to interdisciplinarity (e.g., *trail mix* might be used to describe multidisciplinarity; *smoothie* might be used to describe interdisciplinarity) (Augsburg, 2006).

Klein (1990) also discusses different types of metaphors for disciplinarity and interdisciplinarity. One such disciplinary metaphor might be *territory*. My doctorate is an interdisciplinary degree; it brought together disciplines like psychology and sociology. I also have a graduate certificate in marriage and family therapy. Although I am educated and have knowledge of each of these disciplines, it is unlikely that I would ever be accepted into the psychology department because psychology protects their territory. Equally as unlikely is the idea that I would ever be accepted in the department of sociology. The inverse is not true, however; someone with a psychology degree would be very welcome in a number of interdisciplinary academic departments. Many academic disciplinary departments have a metaphorical, "do not trespass" sign warning others not like them to stay off their property. Having a metaphor that helps others understand interdisciplinarity and your interdisciplinary academic program might be very useful as you as enter the workforce. Be careful that you utilize metaphors that make sense and vividly describe the integrative nature of interdisciplinarity. Some inappropriate metaphors that you should be cautious of are metaphors like bilingualism. A bilingual person would be more like a multidisciplinarian. They can speak multiple languages but there is no integration, there is no synthesis of language (Augsburg, 2006; Klein, 1990). Being able to bring life to the concept of interdisciplinarity is important as you operate in society. Our society, I would argue, needs more interdisciplinarians.

Interdisciplinary Society

Why do we need interdisciplinarians? Our society is made up of many specialists. One problem with having a world of specialists is that each one knows too little about the world in general—each knows a lot about one tree, for example, but very little about how that tree operates in the forest as a whole. Thankfully there are signs that, as a society, we are once again beginning to take a more holistic approach to our own lives and to our planet in general. In this chapter, we will be focusing on the advantages and disadvantages of interdisciplinary study. Hopefully you have already uncovered some of the challenges you will face because you have chosen to complete an interdisciplinary degree program. To be a successful interdisciplinarian, you need to clearly understand, both the disadvantages and advantages of interdisciplinary and integrative studies. You will need to pay attention to the criticism against interdisciplinary studies. There will always be criticisms. Academia, or the universities and colleges that make up higher education, was founded on ironically, the concept of philosophy. We learned about the history of interdisciplinarity in the first part of this text and learned that institutions of higher learning utilized philosophy as an interdisciplinary integration mechanism. We also learned that institutions of higher learning created what we now call academic disciplines. As these academic disciplines created their epistemologies, theories, and research methods, they created for themselves silos of learning. In these academic silos disciplinary perspective reigns supreme, no other discipline could possibly know what they know. These academic silos become a place of comfort for the faculty and students. They learn about a particular discipline and have difficulty communicating with people of other disciplines. They are societies complete with their own language and understanding of the world around them. This separation from and kind of behavior tends to produce experts or specialists in a particular field who can neither understand the world from another perspective nor see the value of interdisciplinary and integrative studies.

Disadvantages and Criticism of Interdisciplinarity

Whether you chose an interdisciplinary degree because of its value or because it seemed the fastest way to graduation, you will need to be able to defend your choice to friends, family members, and potential employers. You will need to able to defend your chosen areas of study and their significance to your career and future plans. Benson (1982) provided five arguments against interdisciplinary studies; serious conceptual confusion, students lacking a mature base in any of the contributing disciplines being integrated, impediments to student's development of a central disciplinary competence, shallow course work, and cost for this type of learning are too high. Interdisciplinary studies practitioners, Benson would argue, lack a coherent, defensible sense of their purpose and they lack the skills necessary to connect meaningful disciplinary insights. Some of the other criticisms are that interdisciplinary projects never get off the ground and the level of scholarship is not very high. Others believe students do not know how to critically think in terms of interdisciplinarity. Still others believe interdisciplinary academic programs are basically a dumping ground for the less than disciplinary competent. For some, interdisciplinary and liberal studies programs are for those who lack direction in their life. Employers will want to know why you did not major in a *normal* degree like engineering, education, biology, hospitality, or psychology. Your parents will want to know what you can do with an interdisciplinary degree when you graduate. There will be no shortage of critics of your interdisciplinary and integrative learning strategies until you are able to clearly articulate the value of this type of learning.

Advantages of Interdisciplinarity

What is the value of an interdisciplinary degree? Why would it be to your advantage to learn skills related to interdisciplinary and integrative learning? Bill Newell, the executive director for the Association of Interdisciplinary Studies, responded to Benson's criticisms of interdisciplinary studies (Newell, 1983). He argued that there is no conceptual confusion. In fact, interdisciplinary studies are about complex problem solving. As interdisciplinarians engage in the interdisciplinary research process, they are seeking out conceptual understanding as it relates to the complex problem under study. Conceptual understanding from different disciplinary insights leads, ultimately, to creating common ground and thus a new conceptual framework for understanding complex problems. Interdisciplinary projects begin with a personal confrontation with the world and all its complexities.

Secondly, Newell argues that interdisciplinarians avoid indoctrination in any single perspective or world view supporting Repko's (2012) notion that we should avoid being seduced by the disciplines. Interdisciplinary and integrative studies teach us the value of considering alternative viewpoints. At some point or another many of us have known someone who refuses to see any idea, problem, or situation from a perspective other than their own. For these types of people there is no amount of evidence or support that will convince them there is another possible perspective. These types of people operate in a disciplinary silo, in their own territory where there is no trespassing allowed. These types of people can be infuriating to work with. Interdisciplinarians on the other hand, see the value in understanding multiple perspectives. Much more than that, they are able to integrate those multiple perspectives to create a holistic understanding of complex problems.

Interdisciplinary and integrative study enables students to be more proactive in their education, and their interdisciplinary degrees are increasingly desirable in the 21st-century workplace. Interdisciplinary academic programs do not teach you how to become a psychologist or an engineer. Arguably neither does the discipline of psychology teach students how to become a psychologist, rather it teaches them the knowledge related to the discipline. Good interdisciplinary programs teach students how to take multiple perspectives and how to synthesize important information from those perspectives in ways that allow holistic solutions to complex problems. Integrative studies allows the learner to go beyond the academic component of their time in college and challenges them to apply their holistic learning to personal experiences. The challenge is to constantly engage in high road knowledge transfer as a way to connect or weave together our life's experiences.

Interdisciplinary and integrative learning can be thoroughly relevant and innovative, enhancing student motivation to engage in the learning process, making these concepts highly effective. Interdisciplinary courses and programs can also be relatively inexpensive and cost saving to universities. For example, instead of having multiple professors teach from their disciplinary perspective, an interdisciplinary course can challenge students to utilize the vast amounts of information already available to provide disciplinary insights of a particular problem or subject. Then one interdisciplinary professor can teach students how to integrate multiple perspectives to create holistic understanding of the problem or subject under study. Students might also work in small groups, bringing their own perspectives and disciplinary insights to the problem. The types of skills students learn in some interdisciplinary/integrative courses provide them with transferable skills that are valuable to potential employers. For example, having to listen to and understand the perspectives of others who may disagree is an opportunity to develop a tolerance for peers. When conflict occurs in studying interdisciplinary problems, overcoming conflict (Leonard, 2012) helps students develop important leadership and collaboration skills. Studying interdisciplinary problems helps students develop a wider knowledge base which, with intentionality, may be transferred to other contexts. Interdisciplinary and integrative learning helps students develop important critical thinking skills.

Interdisciplinary programs allow students to learn from several different disciplines but good interdisciplinary programs also provide a core set of courses that help students learn how to engage in interdisciplinary integration and integrative learning. One thing that sets interdisciplinary and integrative learners apart from disciplinary learners is that they are able to look at any problem from multiple perspectives before arriving at a holistic solution. The source(s) from which they pull—are multifaceted, whereas a disciplinary learner might only be able to draw from their one source of learning. For example, several years ago I was having dinner with a professor friend of mine whose son I would classify as an interdisciplinarian. He has spent all of his life seemingly not knowing exactly what he wanted to do with his life. At least that is the perspective of his parents. He has done a number of different things in his life, he has been a real estate agent, he has worked in churches, worked as a teacher, but he also has a number of fascinating experiences. While we were having dinner I had the opportunity to catch up on his latest venture. He has been involved in this great project to feed families who are unable to feed themselves. At the time, the kind of work they were doing was fairly new, today we see this kind of work being utilized for all kinds of projects. What they had constructed was an aquaponics farm different from hydroponics. Aquaponics is a fascinating interdisciplinary concept. Hydroponics is essentially, the concept of growing plants and vegetables that are planted in seed beds which float in water instead of being planted in the ground. Aquaponics takes the concept a few steps further and adds fish to the growing process. Fish live in the water where the seed beds float. The fish feed on the roots of the plants. The fish in turn fertilize the water which feeds the plants. The plants grow much faster than when planted in the ground. My friend's son was engaged in an interdisciplinary project that was producing vast amounts of healthy meat and vegetables for families who could not afford to feed themselves. Many of these families were unemployed or under employed. Because of the farm, some of these families now had jobs or an increase in family income and they were producing healthy natural food for their families. Hydroponics and aquaponics are just two examples of the many kinds of complex problem solving strategies that interdisciplinarians engage in. On the other hand, a disciplinarian would still be farming traditionally, in some parts of the country, especially in Texas, they would be wondering how to provide water to their farm.

Aquaponics

If you want to know more about aquaponics, check out this video http://www.youtube.com/watch?v=JTwTl0csPdM of a licensed aquaponics farm in Detroit Michigan. Not only are they growing food but they are providing jobs for an underemployed and devastated community. As you watch the video, see if you can tell which disciplinary perspectives they utilize in order to get this project off the ground. Not only is this interdisciplinary project changing their lives, but it is changing the lives of literally thousands of families who cannot afford to feed themselves.

Boonsom/Shutterstock, Inc.

Employers Expectations

Choosing to major in interdisciplinary or liberal studies may not be popular, but the skills students are learning in good interdisciplinary programs are becoming increasingly important to some employers. Fifty-nine percent of employers think universities should provide well-rounded education; that is, broad knowledge and skills that apply to a variety of fields and knowledge and skills in a specific field (AAC&U, 2011). The AAC&U provided a report that discussed the skills employers were looking for in college graduates (Hart, 2006). Overwhelmingly the ability to work well in teams—especially with people different from oneself—is critical for college graduates. Since I have been teaching at the college level I have tried to have students participate in group projects in almost every one of the courses I have taught. Every semester students complain about group work. Group work is difficult. It is difficult because not everyone in the group participates or not everyone gets along. Inevitably someone in the group will get their feelings hurt over something. But group work is a way of life in many careers. Even if one's job is primarily completed as an individual, invariably they must still be able to work with other people. My job as a professor is primarily completed as an individual. I write alone. I teach or lecture alone. I grade papers alone. But the job could not be completed without the help of others. I must be able to work with other faculty members, staff, and students. Yes, at times people in all those positions, including myself, can be difficult to work with. Group work in a college level class is challenging but the transferable skills that can be learned in the activity are invaluable to college graduates entering the workforce. Ninety percent of employers say they are "asking employees to take on more responsibilities and to use a broader set of skills" (AAC&U, 2011).

Employers also expect students to have an understanding of science and technology and how these subjects are used in real-world settings. Nearly 80% think colleges and universities should place more emphasis on helping students develop the ability to apply knowledge and skills to real-world settings through internships or other hands-on experiences. More than 80% of employers believe senior projects, internships and community-based research, and research projects developing students' evidence-based reasoning skills all would help prepare college students for success in today's workplace (AAC&U, 2011). Interdisciplinary and integrative learners are poised to acquire these skills. If they are graduates of a good interdisciplinary program with core integrative courses, they should have developed the skill of interdisciplinary integration and its application. Thus a good interdisciplinarian is able to locate and understand, even if their primary focus of study was not science related, relevant information and its application to real-world problems.

Employers are looking for college graduates that have the ability to write and speak well, the ability to think clearly about complex problems, and the ability to analyze a problem to develop workable solutions. Well-trained interdisciplinarians will have these skills upon graduation. Interdisciplinarians have an understanding of the global context in which work is now done. They have the ability to be creative and innovative in solving complex and real-world problems. Integrative learners who develop their knowledge transfer skills have the ability to apply knowledge and skills in new settings. As all college graduates should, interdisciplinarians should have a strong sense of ethics and integrity.

I understand my bias towards interdisciplinary and integrative learning. However, I truly believe this type of learning has incredible and long-term value to college students who choose to engage in its processes. I hope that you will see the value in the skills related to being an interdisciplinary and integrative learner, those of being a critical thinker, asking meaningful questions, and finding the connections between what you are learning in academia and how it applies to your life.

Characteristics of Interdisciplinarians

Interdisciplinarians have certain characteristics. They have a different type of educational experience that provide them with the opportunity to develop important skills that can easily be transferred and applied to one's career and future plans. Interdisciplinarians are competent and have broad interests. They are typically self-secure with their knowledge, skills, and abilities. Repko and Welch (2005) discuss characteristics and traits that interdisciplinarians typically have. "Students drawn to interdisciplinary studies have an unusual love of learning, they're curious beyond the average about the world they live in and welcome opportunities to view the world from as many perspectives as possible" (Repko & Welch, 2005, p. 23). Interdisciplinarians have a **love of learning** and become **lifelong learners**. If you find yourself in the position of having chosen an interdisciplinary degree by default, as a way to get out of college, having a love of learning is one way to reframe your academic experience in a more positive light. Interdisciplinarians love to learn. Perhaps you had difficulty choosing a major, transferring multiple times, from major to major to major to major, until finding yourself in an interdisciplinary degree program. Perhaps you were frustrated with feeling forced into an interdisciplinary experience. Maybe your parents were really frustrated with that pathway. But by engaging in some self-reflective activities for a moment, consider that your pathway was right all along. That the difficulty you had in choosing a major or committing to a major was because you are at heart an interdisciplinarian but did not realize it. This is a much different perspective on academic learning. It is not because you could not commit or do well in particular majors; rather you have varied interests in multiple learning opportunities. Interdisciplinary degree programs at universities across the country provide a structure for those students who love learning different perspectives. Repko and Welch (2005) also discuss the fact that interdisciplinarians have an **appreciation of diversity**. Interdisciplinarians have respect for people holding different views, devoted to different favored traditions, and coming from different cultural and racial backgrounds. Interdisciplinarians are willing to see beyond the surface, to be open minded about differences in opinion and diversity. They are able to synthesize issues of diversity in ways that help create comprehensive understanding of important global issues.

Interdisciplinarians have a strong ability to **communicate effectively** to multiple audiences. "Each discipline has not only its own set of skills and knowledge but also its own language that it uses to describe its concepts, assumptions, and theories" (Repko & Welch, 2005, p. 26). One must be able to understand topics that seem foreign and unfamiliar by using prior knowledge and skills; that is, low road and high road transfer. This may require that we have the ability to **think abstractly**. "The interdisciplinarian must integrate various perspectives relevant to the problem and, ideally, should be able to express this new understanding symbolically in terms of a metaphor" (Repko & Welch, 2005, p. 26) Interdisciplinarians are people who hold specific traits and skills that allow them to be extremely well-rounded and versed in many subjects. Interdisciplinarians are interested in the world around them. They love to learn about new things, often times with a passion that many people find themselves dedicating only to their most favorite subject.

Interdisciplinary and integrative learning is a fascinating way to live life. It allows us to have unique experiences as we go about our day. I have discussed a number of experiences I have had in my life but there are also small things that I learn about, sometimes out of interest and other times out of necessity. Yes there are disadvantages to being an interdisciplinarian. You will almost always have to explain and defend your interdisciplinary academic experience. You will need to find ways to describe who you are to potential employers. Understanding more about what employers are expecting from college graduates and typical characteristics of interdisciplinarians should help you begin to develop your interdisciplinary story.

References

AAC&U. (2011). The LEAP vision for learning: Outcomes, practices, impact, and employers' views. Washington, DC: Association of Amercian Colleges and Universities.

Augsburg, T. (2006). *Becoming interdisciplinary: An introduction to interdisciplinary studies* (2nd ed.). Dubuque, IA: Kendall Hunt.

Benson, T. C. (1982). Five arguments against interdisciplinary studies. *Issues in Integrative Studies, 1*(1), 38–48.

Hart, P. (2006). How should colleges prepare students to succeed in today's global economy? Washington, DC: The Association of American Colleges and Universities.

Klein, J. T. (1990). *Interdisciplinarity: history, theory, & practice.* Detroit, MI: Wayne State University Press.

Leonard, J. B. (2012). Integrative learning: A grounded theory. *Issues in Integrative Studies* (30), 48–74.

Newell, W. H. (1983). The case for interdisciplinary studies. *Issues in Integrative Studies, 2,* 1–19.

Repko, A. F. (2012). *Interdisciplinary research: Process and theory* (2nd ed.). Thousand Oaks, CA: Sage.

Repko, A. F., & Welch, J. (2005). *Interdisciplinary practice: A student guide to research and writing.* Boston, MA: Pearson Custom Publishing.

CHAPTER 10

Issues on Global Perspectives and Team Leadership

In the previous chapter, we discussed the advantages and characteristics of interdisciplinarians as well as employers' expectations of college graduates. Two expectations that employers have of college graduates that may deserve more attention are the ability to view problems in terms of a global economy and being able to work well in teams. These abilities are also general characteristics of interdisciplinarians. Interdisciplinarians, as we previously discussed, have an appreciation for diversity; thus, perspectives from multiple viewpoints are important when coming in contact with complex problems. Up until this point we have framed our discussion around the learning that primarily happens in an academic setting. However, interdisciplinary and integrative learning has perhaps, more value outside of the confines of academia.

Globalization

The world in which we live is becoming increasing globalized. **Globalization** is defined as "the process of increasing interconnectedness between societies such that events in one part of the world more and more have effects on people and societies far away" (Baylis & Smith, 1997, p. 7). Because the world is increasing in its interconnectedness what can students do to prepare themselves to live and work in such a society? The American Association of Colleges and Universities (AAC&U) provides several suggestions that would be of benefit to students. They noted, students should acquire knowledge of human cultures and the physical and natural world, practice intellectual and practical skills (i.e., critical thinking, teamwork, and problem solving), be actively involved in personal and social responsibility, and demonstrate application of these skills and knowledge through integrative learning (AAC&U, 2007). While some individuals choose not to take notice of the interconnectedness of the world, the truth is, what happens in one part of the world may have a significant impact in their microsystem. Globalization can be separated into four categories; exponential increases in international economic transaction, integration of internal/global economic decision making, strengthened political international governmental organization, and increases in international nongovernmental contracts and communication.

As students who are early in their careers or soon to launch into their first career, it is important that you consider how you will play a role in the continued globalization of the world.

Global Diversity

It is important then, that interdisciplinary and integrative learners have an understanding of different perspectives in the world and how it relates to **global diversity**. It is important to note that global diversity is to consider the differences between the individuals and people groups that comprise humanity. These differences may include race but diversity is much more than that. Diversity includes differences in opinion, thought, ethnicity, culture, geographic location, and more. Do not be trapped into thinking diversity is just about race, it is not. There are several reactions to diversity that you should consider. The first is **ethnocentrism** which is "judging the customs of another culture according to standards of your own" (Kelleher & Klein, 2011, p. 38). This is perhaps the most common reaction to diversity as universally, children are raised to value their own culture over that of another. As a result of ethnocentrism we may learn to see other cultures as wrong or deficient in some way. One solution to ethnocentricity is the concept of **cultural relativity** which suggests that the actions of people within a culture should be evaluated according to the rules of their own culture (p. 38). **Racism** and **sexism** are judgments people make based on race or biological differences. Some individuals and people groups view other races and genders as inferior. These kinds of inferiority judgments distort the understanding one may have of the world and its cultures. This may bring up the question of whether **human rights** are inherently possessed by all or are there some rights that override cultural traditions and state sovereignty? Since 1948, the United Nations has supported 60 human rights that include: life, liberty, and freedom of movement, freedom from slavery, freedom of religion, education, expression, and marriage. Unfortunately, abstract laws for human rights do not always lead to a reality for cultures. Ethnicity, class, religion, and region all influence the learning of values and manners of thinking. These differing sets of ideas are called **alternative perspectives**. Global diversity does not ask what is right and wrong, but *how* and *why* people approach issues differently. Even if you were raised from birth in America your cultural values may be very different from the person who you are sitting next to. Even though you lived down the street from your best friend you might have had two different experiences in regards to culture, religion, and the values that your families taught the both of you.

As you engage in complex problem solving in terms of global and social issues, it is important for interdisciplinary and integrative learners to view them through the lens of the culture related to the issue. Work to develop multiple lenses for which to view complex global and social issues. People approach issues differently, maybe one person's primary area of study is nutrition interested in the chemistry of proper nutrition. How would a nutritionist look at issues in education, as opposed to someone whose background is in psychology interested in human behavior? Not only does their disciplinary perspective make a difference in how they will view a problem but so will the diversity of their culture.

Global Primacy

Global primacy is the belief that the world is divided into specific political and economic entities (Kelleher & Klein, 2011). Those who embrace this concept believe that the more backward cultures will disappear when individuals recognize the benefits of the more advanced cultures and voluntarily change their ways. They also encourage further social integration of the world's people. I sometimes consider this concept in terms of a one world government, or one world system; that even though we are separated by miles and miles, separated by oceans, separated by continents, the world should have one currency, one government, and that everyone, despite their cultural values would operate in the same way. Global primacy places major value on individuals rather than on groups, or people, or systems of government.

Here are some other terms related to globalization you should familiarize yourself with. The first is **assimilation**, where over time people will give up the customs of their inferior cultures to become full members of superior cultures. At one time America was considered the **melting pot,** which is the idea that immigrants would come to the United States and assimilate their cultures, values, and beliefs into the American way of life. Those who would come to America were expected to give up previous values, ideas, and beliefs. Some believed that to assimilate to American culture would lead to the destruction of their own. **Ethnocide** is the destruction of a culture. Perhaps the fear of ethnocide has led many towards the concept of **acculturation,** which is to modify cultural upbringing to adjust to a new culture (Kelleher & Klein, 2011). Americans are providing more and more opportunities for acculturation and focusing less on assimilation. Something as simple as governmental signage being required with both the English and Spanish language is an example of acculturation. No longer are people being required to learn and speak fluently in the English language. With every new school year, we fill out a lot of paperwork for our children to go to school. One side of the form is written in English and on the other side is written in Spanish. We notice this more in some states where the population is more diverse. It seems that America is acculturating. Individuals and families moving to this country are bringing their culture with them, and American culture has adapted to new ways of operating in this globalized world. Acculturation is perhaps a foreshadowing of things to come. **Syncretism**, for example, is the mixing of cultural ideas from different sources in order to create a new reality (Kelleher & Klein, 2011). This type of perspective recognizes that the creation of a new global reality in which everyone will share in mutually satisfying cultures is a difficult challenge but worthwhile.

Interdisciplinary and integrative learners are global thinkers; they view the world and its complexity through multiple lenses. These lenses are not just disciplinary lenses, but they are ethnic and cultural having a tolerance for diversity of thought and engagement with the world. Being able to engage in complex problem solving not only requires a global perspective, but employers expect college graduates to be able to work well in teams.

Interdisciplinary Teams

A team is a "specialized group with a performance objective or goal that requires coordinating activity" (Klein, 2005, p. 23). Interdisciplinary teams operate in more complex environments. One example of an interdisciplinary team is the groups of people who worked on the Manhattan Project. It was a research and development project that produced the first atomic bombs. This project involved multiple teams, multiple perspectives, all working together to come up with a solution to a complex problem. Interdisciplinary teams are open, not closed, systems; we briefly discussed systems theory in a previous chapter. **Open systems** are those that allow interactions between its internal elements and the environment (Von Bertalanffy, 1956). Interdisciplinary teams are also heterogeneous but interconnected (Klein, 2005). There are also two types of interdisciplinary teams, narrow and broad. Narrow interdisciplinary teams are exemplified by a team, composed of those with the same paradigm methods and shared knowledge, while broad interdisciplinary teams are exemplified by groups composed of many disciplines that are dispersed across different organizations, different paradigms, methods, and knowledge, all of which complicate communication (Klein, 2005). There are several other types of teams Klein discusses (i.e., consensus and boiler room teams). They embody truer teamwork because a proposed leader is in charge but the entire team works through every key issue of the complex problem. As you have the opportunity to work in interdisciplinary teams, consider the diversity of their backgrounds and disciplinary orientation. If you are the leader of the group, consider how you will bring the team together. Where does *common ground* exist between the individuals of the group? How can you provide *synthesis* of the group members? Remember these two terms; previously we discussed them in the context of interdisciplinary research but they are applicable here as well. Not only can interdisciplinary and integrative learners engage in complex problem solving, but they can put together and integrate teams that are best suited to the task. Almost all the literature pertaining to group and team work suggests that small groups with stable membership are the most integrative. As you work to create your own interdisciplinary team to work on large problems, consider having small break-out teams, each one with their own leader, each one working on parts of the solution to the complex problem or issue. Consider again the Manhattan Project where there was a small group of leaders that were working on the overall objectives and goals of the project, but each one of those leaders had smaller groups of teams where they dealt with more specific and key areas of the whole project. Klein (2005) uses the terms *ringmaster* and *gatekeeper* as metaphors for interdisciplinary team leaders. A ring master at the circus, for example, is responsible for the coordination of all that is happening in each ring of the circus and bringing them together in such a way that spectators get a complete show.

Problems in Interdisciplinary Teamwork

As you might imagine based on our previous discussion, there are problems with engaging in interdisciplinary teamwork. We previously discussed the concept of disciplinary territory and the idea of operating within a silo of information. Individuals that have strong proclivities toward their disciplinary training may engage in turf battles and be resistant to innovation. They may be mistrustful and insecure as they operate within the team environment. Leonard (2012) offered some strategies for how to overcome conflict when working towards integration. Team members may lack integrative skills, systems thinking, and familiarity with the concepts of interdisciplinarity. Conflict may arise that is associated with both technical and interpersonal issues. People bring excess organizational baggage including perceptions of others, status, pre-conceived role ideas, and differing understanding of the problem. The ultimate goal is to overcome the disciplinary issues in such a way as to arrive at a new understanding of the complex problem. Consider some skills and abilities you will need to overcome some of the barriers to interdisciplinary teamwork.

Peter Lencioni (2002) discusses what he calls the five dysfunctions of a team; the absence of trust, fear of conflict, lack of commitment, avoidance of accountability, and inattention to results. Relate these dysfunctions to some of the groups you may have participated in at some point. When people do not trust each other, they do not talk to each other or they communicate in half-truths and vagaries. It is important as a foundation for teams to work together to establish trust among one another.

People who have a fear of conflict are usually engaged in an artificial harmony. They operate in such a way as to not cause any waves or disruptions in the group. They do not want anybody in the group to become upset. Conflict, unfortunately, has a negative connotation. But there is such a thing as good conflict. If everyone on a team always agrees with one another, the likelihood of that group ever producing anything more than what they are currently doing is severely diminished. There needs to be healthy conflict when working together in a group in such a way that true harmony is produced. True harmony exists when group members are able to disagree in a safe environment, where their opinions are valued, and the group leader works toward integrating information.

Lack of commitment is an issue for any team but especially interdisciplinary teams. When a lack of commitment exists there is a cloud of ambiguity among team members. Remember that one student in your class groups that would never commitment to anything? They operated as an ambiguous team member; they might show up to the group meetings but would never do their part. These kinds of people also try to avoid accountability. These types of people have a low standard for their work or make excuses for not doing their work. At the top of Lencioni's (2002) pyramid of dysfunction is the concept of intention to results. These people tend to be more worried about their status or their ego in the group than the work itself.

Interdisciplinary teams are status systems that reflect external hierarchies in disciplinary chauvinism. There are status barriers, or barriers based on gender, race, cultural backgrounds, and disciplinary pecking orders. There are many barriers to engaging in good interdisciplinary teamwork, and we have only discussed a few of them. Interdisciplinary and integrative learners work towards overcoming barriers of any kind.

References

AAC&U. (2007). College learning for the new global century. Washington, DC: Association of American Colleges and Universities.

Baylis, J., & Smith, S. (1997). *The globalization of world politics: An introduction to international relations.* New York: Oxford University Press.

Kelleher, A., & Klein, L. (2011). *Global perspectives* (4th ed.). Boston: Pearson.

Klein, J. T. (2005). Interdisciplinary teamwork: The dynamics of collaboration and integration. In S. J. Derry & C. D. Schunn (Eds.), *Interdisciplinary collaboration: An emerging cognitive science* (pp. 23–50). New York, NY: Psychology Press.

Lencioni, P. (2002). *The five dysfunctions of a team: A leadership fable.* San Francisco: Jossey-Bass.

Leonard, J. B. (2012). Integrative learning: A grounded theory. *Issues in Integrative Studies* (30), 48–74.

Von Bertalanffy, L. (1956). General system theory. *General systems, 1*(1), 11–17.

CHAPTER 11

Constructing Interdisciplinarity

In this part of the textbook, we have been discussing priorities of interdisciplinary and integrative learners. In Chapter 9, we discussed characteristics of interdisciplinarians, especially those important to employers. In Chapter 10, we expounded on two important priorities for interdisciplinarians and employers, the expectation that college graduates are able to work successfully in teams and approach problems from a global perspective. This chapter will focus on an important intrinsic concept for the interdisciplinarian that is constructing their interdisciplinarity. With this chapter we take a further step back from interdisciplinary research and problem solving and press further into the essence and behavior of the interdisciplinarian. We will do this by framing our discussion around the concept of construing continuity, considering the family life cycle, and telling our interdisciplinary story.

Bateson (1994) eloquently discusses the concept of construing continuity in the telling of her own story. To disciplinarians our work and the way we live our life often seems disconnected, disjointed, gone awry, or lacking direction. If you are a current college student, you may have experienced this sentiment when your family found out you were completing an interdisciplinary degree program. They probably asked why or what will you do with such a degree. You may recognize your own life as being disjointed or perhaps lacking direction. It is my intent, in this chapter, to argue that your life is not disjointed or lacking direction. Rather you have always been an interdisciplinarian who lacked proper construction in continuity. One way we can define *construe* is to mean interpret. Because interdisciplinarians operate in the world a little differently than disciplinarians, another important skill we can develop is to help people interpret the way in which we see and operate in the world as an alternative perspective or continuity. That means that we must interpret the *common ground* between our life's experiences in such a way that not only we can make sense of our world but that others might also. When our experiences in life seem disconnected or discontinuous, it can create stress, anxiety, and provide a sense of disillusionment that somehow we have not lived our life properly. I believe Bateson argues that a disillusioned perspective of life should be modified. In other words, our life cannot be viewed as one continuous perfect trajectory. Instead we construe a perspective that takes notice of the trajectory but also the stopping points or discontinuities in our life.

The Family Life Cycle

In this section we will discuss the family life cycle in the context of Bateson's concept of construing continuity. In the next section we will more fully discuss construing continuity. The concept of the family life cycle comes from marriage and family therapy and systems background and is a theoretical model that helps us understand how families develop and respond to changes familial changes over time. The family is considered a system moving through time. Problems are framed by the formative course of our family's past, the present tasks that one is trying to master, and the future to which one aspires. As part of the family life cycle, cultural differences and changes in the family structure are important considerations (McGoldrick, Carter, & Garcia-Preto, 2011). As discussed in the previous chapter, there are larger, more global issues that affect how we live life. McGoldrick et al. (2011) describe seven stages of the family life cycle:

1. Leaving Home: Emerging Adults
2. Joining of Families Through Marriage/Union
3. Families with Young Children
4. Families with Adolescents
5. Launching Children and Moving on in Midlife
6. Families in Late Middle Age
7. Families Nearing the End of Life

Within each of these stages there exists an emotional process of transition and second order changes in family status required to proceed developmentally. For example, families with adolescents experience a shift in the parent–child relationships that permits the adolescent to move in and out of the system. Parents then must increase the flexibility of the family boundaries to permit expressed independence of the child. While at the same time parents may be caring for their parents. At each one of these stages individuals within the system as well as the system itself should be working toward successfully negotiating change or discontinuity.

There are many examples of change or discontinuity that families will experience. That human beings are living longer affects many aspects of society. For example, your children will likely have access, even if for short time, to their grandparents, great grandparents, and perhaps even their great, great grandparents. The structure of *family* has been changing over time; families are not comprised of the concept of the nuclear family—mother, father, and two children. Divorce, co-habitation choices, single parent choices, gay and lesbian families make for different family configurations across a lifespan that have an effect on the family life cycle. While the configuration of families is changing in our society, so are individuals. People are in general more educated than in the recent past. They are living longer than in the recent past. People have access to much more information than in the past. Advances in technology and the way in which we use it also has an effect on our family.

We can think of change happening on two different axes, the horizontal and the vertical. The **vertical axis** includes the issues that seem more continuous in nature. These are those familiar influences in your life such as family values, beliefs, heritage, and culture. We often consider these issues to remain fairly constant over time. Very rarely do family values change over time. The **horizontal axis** includes issues that may seem more discontinuous. For example, relationship with others, events in your life like losing a significant other, graduating from high school, losing a job, having a baby, getting married. As people go through life they experience these discontinuous episodes—birth, marriage, divorce, death, job changes, education, etc. These episodes often create stress which can have both a positive and negative effects. As a marriage and family therapist, my experience has been that many people tend to get bogged down in thinking about these normal life transitions from a negative perspective which adds to their stress. When stress becomes overwhelming dysfunctional behavior usually follows. What is helpful is to interpret or construe continuity within these lifecycle transitions. Certainly, it is a negative experience to lose a job. Losing a job can bring with it all kinds of short- and long-term negative effects. However, as the life cycle continues one can purposefully attempt to locate the continuity in the transition. They can reframe the experience in a positive way. As they decrease their stress levels they can also work toward **homeostasis** or stability of their own lives and the family system in response to change.

The concepts of place and time are also important as you consider how to interpret your own development as an interdisciplinarian. Consider some of the historical and cultural events that are relevant to your development as opposed to your parents and grandparents. Perhaps you have never considered this, but almost everyone born after 2002 in the United States either does not know about or understand the significance of the events of 9/11. They do not understand how those events on 9/11 relate to the wars in Iraq and Afghanistan, even if their parents may be serving in the military. Many heterosexuals over the age of 65 do not appreciate or understand gay and lesbian lifestyles and are against same-sex marriage. Many people over the age of 75 have never used a computer and find limited uses for it in their life. In the 1950s, the standard home size was 1,100 square foot. Today, the standard home size is twice that. In contrast, the family size is getting smaller. So houses are getting bigger but the family size is getting smaller. Societies change over time and our place, or where we belong, in society also changes. Our perspective of change and how we operate within it changes. Consider some of the following: there are now 7.8 million couples living together without being married, more than double the 2.9 million from 1996. Married households make up 49% of all households, down from 71% in 1970. The proportion of households headed by white non-Hispanic adults stands at 69% this year, down 8% from 75% in 2000. Fifty-two percent of married couples have both husbands and wives in the labor force, which is down slightly from 56% in 2000. The percentage of stay home parents who are fathers has grown from 1.6% in 1994 to 3.6% in 2014. Among married couples, parents with children younger than age 15, the percentage of stay-at-home mothers is estimated to be 24%. Eighty-five percent of single race Asian children live with two parents whether married or not; the proportion falls to 77% among single race White non-Hispanic children, 66% of Hispanic children, and 38% of single raised African-American children. Families are changing. You probably identify with any number of the changes mentioned. Maybe your parents are divorced. Maybe you were raised in a single family home or by someone who was not your biological parent, or by a gay or lesbian couple. Perhaps you have experienced other changes over the course of your life thus far that have had a significant impact on you. Consider how the changing context of family is important or not important as you interpret your interdisciplinary story. Tell the story of where you belong.

Another concept related to the family life cycle is home or homeplace. **Homeplace** symbolizes the importance of belonging. How one defines or describes their homeplace is diverse. The phrase "home is where the heart is" is appropriate to represent the idea of homeplace. In terms of family where do you feel like you belong? In terms of your education, what group do you feel like you belong to? Homeplace is an essential part of our cultural and individual identity. The notion that we *belong* provides for a type of resilience that helps us deal with the injustices of society or family. Homeplace is a way for us to develop and express family values. It is the place where we acknowledge forces in history that have made us strong. It is a place of resistance, a place that challenges us to become who we will be. Perhaps you can remember a time, growing up, where you were trying to become your own person, make some of your own decisions about life but your parents prevented you from going your own way. This resistance is part of the family life cycle that requires flexibility in boundaries. Homeplace is a site for confrontation and learning to negotiate with the world as you become an adult. It is a place of physical, spiritual, and emotional connection. It is not necessarily the home where you were raised, but it is the place that calls to you, draws you home. It can also be a community on multiple levels of the human system. Homeplace can bridge the gap between the private and public.

Construing Continuity

Most people focus primarily on the discontinuities and changes in life rather than those experiences that provide continuity. Bateson (1994, 2001) discusses the need for **flexibility** or reinvention as people consider both the continuities and discontinuities of life.

> I believe in the need for multiple models . . . to weave something new from many different threads . . . When we speak to our children about our own lives we tend to reshape our pasts to give them an illusory look of purpose. But our children are unlikely to be able to define their goals and then live happily ever after. Instead, they will need to reinvent themselves again and again in response to a changing environment. Once you begin to see these . . . multiple commitments and multiple beginnings as an emerging pattern rather than an aberration,...the models for that reinvention . . . are not fixed but . . . evolve from day to day. (Bateson, 2001, pp. 16–77)

Instead of looking at our life as a single trajectory, Bateson (1994) encourages us to view it, on a rising curve or even a zigzag line, flexible thinking helps us to see our life as a rising spiral with multiple potential pathways (see Figure 11.1).

We experience changing rules and relationships as we go throughout life. We experience all kinds of transitions which may lead to different pathways. Our identity evolves over time. It adapts according to the influences in our life. We adapt, reinvent ourselves, and shift our identities. This is being flexible as we encounter discontinuities. Some may look at shifting identities

FIGURE 11.1   Rising Spiral

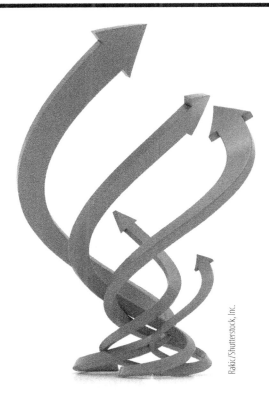

Rakic/Shutterstock, Inc.

as becoming a new person. Bateson (1994) would argue that this shifting is not becoming a new person, but rather weaving a particular influence into the fabric of our life in a way that makes sense. We all experience discontinuity, we all experience transition, we all experience change. It is how we assimilate those changes into our life that makes a difference in whether our further development is healthy. Not only do interdisciplinarians need to integrate a sense of who we are vertically and horizontally, our healthy existence to some extent depends on whether we can construe continuity within the discontinuity of our life.

As you consider how you will interpret yourself as an interdisciplinarian, consider the characteristics and skills important to interdisciplinarity. Consider the importance of differences, diversity, and discontinuities. Remember interdisciplinarians tend to celebrate diversity. Ask important questions about who you are. Do you have a diverse background? How do you celebrate diversity in your own life, in the context of your family? Are there behavioral or emotional attributes that are important to you as an interdisciplinarian? Think about your education and how it relates to your career and future plans. Think about the stages of life, your experiences, and the places in your life that are either continuous or discontinuous. We tend to think so much about the discontinuities instead of working to focus on the continuities in your relationship with family, significant others, and long-term friends. Search for continuity in patterns of behavior. Although your context or environment changes and time changes, patterns of behavior largely remain the same over time. Look for continuity in your identity of self. How you describe yourself may change over time as different issues become more important but a thread of continuity remains.

I have shared quite a bit about my personal life in this text as examples of interdisciplinarity and integrative learning. Here is another example; on my father's side, my great grandfather and my grandfather were farmers. My dad grew up and was trained to be a farmer, but when he started his family he decided to be a mechanic instead. My grandfather may have looked at that decision as being discontinuous to the family way of life. But my dad may have looked at that decision as continuous because his focus as a mechanic was agricultural mechanics. Although he may not have realized it, he was using low-road transfer to transfer his knowledge from working on the farm, driving tractors, and repairing them when they were broken, to being a mechanic who then started an agricultural repair shop. In my family, I am a first generation college graduate; no one in my immediate family has graduated from college. My college education could be looked at as a discontinuous point in my life cycle. But it could also be looked at as a continuous thread. Although my family is not formally educated, they are educated. My family has a long history of living by the motto attributed to President Theodore Roosevelt, "If anyone asks you to do something tell them yes then get busy learning how to do it." For many of you, your decisions have led you down a path that could be construed as continuous or discontinuous depending on who you ask. Maybe you have a long history of the engineers in your family but you chose a different path. While your family may see that decision as discontinuous you may be able to find the connections and interpret your decision as continuous instead. The goal, the challenge, as we construct our interdisciplinarity, is to find the thread that weaves together our discontinuities.

Constructing Your Story

This section will help us make a transition between Part III and Part IV of the text. In Part III we have been focusing on priorities of interdisciplinarians. In Part IV our focus will be on preparing for graduation. So in this final section it is important that we discuss how you will construct your interdisciplinary story. How will you answer the question that many employers will ask, 'Tell me about yourself'? It is one of the first questions that you will be asked in almost every job interview you have. It may also be the first question you receive in interviews for graduate school. Perhaps the question is in written form on an application. Perhaps it is part of a conversation that you have with someone. Without fail you will be asked some variation of this question, 'Tell me about yourself?' You will likely also have to explain your interdisciplinary or liberal arts degree and the areas of study you chose to focus on. How are you going to utilize your learning and apply it to your life? You have likely had these types of questions posed to you already, perhaps by your parents, a significant other, or an employer.

The first step to constructing your interdisciplinary story is to define interdisciplinarity in the context of your audience. Second, having a metaphor that is relevant to the audience can help people understand the concept of interdisciplinarity. The way you define interdisciplinarity should also be framed around the value of interdisciplinary or liberal arts education and your interdisciplinary experiences in college. Your metaphor should be creative and related to your own life experiences. It will have much more meaning to you and you will be able to communicate much more effectively to your audience. Third, tell your story in terms of your skills, abilities, and interdisciplinary characteristics. In particular is that interdisciplinarians are lifelong learners. They have a love of learning which may prevent them from being experts or the authority in any one field, but they have the ability to transfer knowledge from one context to another.

One thing that I have noticed about people in general is that they are storytellers. Some are better at it than others but almost everyone tells stories. As you think ahead, towards graduation, it is important for you to consider the types of stories that you will tell about your interdisciplinary self, your education, and your work experiences. You should be able to consider the interdisciplinary nature of your degree, the content of your learning, the connections between your areas of study, and be able to connect them to your story while discussing your skills and abilities. It is vital that you find the thread or threads that weave your story together. Consider the one thing that brings all three of these areas of study together. Consider how you will reinvent yourself or shift your identity toward your career goals.

Your story or personal narrative needs to be deeply true and so engaging, so that listeners feel that they have a stake in your success. Make sure that your story illustrates that you have a life that lends itself to being interdisciplinary. Talk about your interdisciplinary characteristics, your skills, your self-reflexivity, and your self-identity. You should be able to discuss your chosen areas of study in a way that makes sense and makes connections to your career choice.

As you think about what stories you might tell, follow some of these general guidelines. Make sure that you assume a general reader who does not know you personally. Do not dwell on the negative or discontinuous experience. Instead, develop the continuities within discontinuous experiences. Interdisciplinary education can be very positive and valuable to your career and future plans, but you must be able to interpret your interdisciplinarity in a way that makes sense to your audience.

References

Bateson, M. C. (1994). *Peripheral visions: Learning along the way.* Canada: HarperCollins.

Bateson, M. C. (2001). *Composing a life.* New York: Grove Press.

McGoldrick, M., Carter, B. L., & Garcia-Preto, N. (Eds.). (2011). *The expanded family life cycle: Individual, family, and social perspectives* (4th ed.). Boston: Allyn & Bacon.

PART IV

Interdisciplinary
Portfolios

CHAPTER 12

The Value of Interdisciplinary Studies

So much has already been written about interdisciplinary and integrative studies. One might already see the inherent value of each in their own life. The critics of interdisciplinarity and integrative learning are plentiful. Many of those critics are academicians that have a myopic focus on research and learning. Other critics are those that have little understanding of what it means to be interdisciplinary. In part we will discuss how to develop your portfolio. Part of your portfolio of course is having the ability to tell your story, which we discussed in the previous chapter. As you tell that story critics of interdisciplinarity and others in your life who care about you will want to know the value of this type of degree program, which we will discuss in this chapter. Chapter 13 discusses the mechanics of developing interdisciplinary portfolios. Many employers will want you to create some type of portfolio as part of the interviewing process. At other times having a portfolio will make the job search process easier for you. In Chapter 14, we will discuss resumes, an essential part of any job search and should be a major part of your portfolio. We will wrap up Part IV and this text book by discussing your next steps whether that be graduation and moving into your first career or attending graduate school. I will endeavor to pass on some incredible advice I received and offer some advice from observations I have made.

A Systemic Complex Problem

When we discuss the value of interdisciplinary and integrative learning, it is first helpful to understand the problems associated with them. We have already discussed several problems with interdisciplinary and integrative learning. We referenced Benson's (1982) five arguments against interdisciplinary studies. We also discussed problems with describing interdisciplinary and integrative learning, working in teams, overcoming bias, creating common ground, and more.

But the problem with interdisciplinary and integrative studies might better be looked at as a systemic complex problem. I am not advocating that the disciplines should not exist. Interdisciplinarity could not exist without the disciplines. But I am arguing that learning has changed over the course of time. We learned in the first part of this text that from what we know about early learning, it was essentially integrative in nature. There was one teacher to teach a group of students, although they may have learned several "subjects" there is little doubt that the teacher was polymathic and had knowledge of all the subjects taught. Before education to the masses existed, individuals learned from a "master." This master had the ability to teach many subjects and help the student apply that learning to life. One example we used was that of Leonardo da Vinci, a prolific polymathist. As time went on there was a need for specialists, which we have already discussed. The need for specialists required both the teacher and student to focus their attention on one subject, to know as much as they possibly could about that subject and how they might apply it to life in their context. This type of learner became the expert, passing on knowledge to those who needed access to it while also teaching others to become an expert. Thus the disciplines were born; no longer would the learner look at a problem from a polymathic point of view but they would now see their world from the perspective of their training. There is nothing wrong with this type of learning and operation in the world, we still need specialists. However, what happens when one encounters a complex problem? We are forced to accept the disciplinary perspective of the problem. Or with people who are trained to be integrative and interdisciplinary learners, we might utilize multiple disciplinary perspectives to provide a holistic perspective of a problem.

Universities and other institutions of learning are not set up for teaching from an integrative perspective. In United States primary schools, kindergarten through third grade, students largely remain in the same classroom with the same teacher all day. This teacher is expected to train them in writing, reading, math, science, and music, perhaps the only time the students are not with that teacher is when they go to physical education. The specific teaching methods matter, but in general, this is an integrative learning environment. For some reason, somewhere around fourth or fifth grades teaching becomes disciplinary for the student. Until they finish formal education, which may include graduate school, students are taught from a disciplinary perspective and the training of teachers is also disciplinary. In the real world, the problems we encounter are not disciplinary. Parenting is not disciplinary, owning a home is not disciplinary, working in a career is not disciplinary. Yes, in all these, one must have some knowledge of disciplines, but they must also be able to draw on information from other perspectives.

As stated previously, the concepts of interdisciplinary and integrative learning are not new. They have both been a part of the university environment before. Academicians typically consider this type of learning Liberal Studies, which was very popular in the 1960s and '70s In recent years, interdisciplinary studies has become more of a focus for some universities in the U.S. and around the world. However, there exists significant disciplinary barriers that proliferate isolation of knowledge. Disciplinary epistemologies are often incompatible with one another which makes solving complex problems an issue. Structural barriers divide colleges and departments in such way that limits communication between students and teachers, teachers, and administrators. A student may take a class in the psychology department that focuses on human development and another course in the education department that focuses on classroom management. The student would benefit greatly from collaboration between the teachers of these two courses but because these two courses are in different departments and likely different colleges, these two teachers probably do not know each other or consider how an integrative learning environment might help this student. We also know that colleges and departments work directly against each other in competition for resources, usually in terms of student enrollment for tuition and fee dollars. The problem is complex. I believe we need the disciplines, experts in particular fields have added value to our society and way of life but at what cost.

The Need for Interdisciplinary Studies

We have already implicitly discussed the many benefits to interdisciplinary and integrative learning. In Chapter 9, we referenced Newell's (1983) response to Benson's criticism of interdisciplinary studies. We need interdisciplinarians to overcome some of the problems of having too many experts. Promoting interdisciplinary and integrative learning in institutions of higher education would promote the idea that a holistic understanding of many of the world's problems would, perhaps, help create new pioneers and innovators that would help solve global problems.

Newell (2007) argued that our

> Students will face challenges in the next several decades unlike those in the past [where] small events on one part of the planet and in one sphere of human existence can now end up having large and relatively rapid effects on other parts of the planet and in other spheres of human existence.

The world in which we live in is not disciplinary. One cannot successfully operate in this world from a single perspective. The world is complex, even in smaller ecological systems like small towns or even families, problems are complex and not easily solved or understood using a single perspective. While academic disciplines are important and necessary, they are not adequate for understanding complex problems. Newell (2007) argues that interdisciplinarity is pragmatic "in a world characterized by complex problems."

Integrative Learning

The challenge for the interdisciplinarian is to view the disciplines from the relevancy they add to real world problems. Using integrative learning can help students overcome the tendency to preserve preconceived ideas about how the world works. As a reminder, Leonard (2012) discovered four forms of integration that interdisciplinary students engage in: application, comparison, understanding context, and synthesis where students applied what they were learning to multiple contexts. Integrative learning is a process where students bridge curricular and co-curricular activities, explore and make connections across their general education curriculum and their major focus of study, and synthesize previous learning with new. Newell (2007) conceptualized interdisciplinarity as the bridge between the higher education and the real world.

Value Defined

College degrees are typically valued in terms of how much money a graduate can make in the related field. Thus some of the highly *valued* degrees are in the field of business, economics, engineering, and medicine. The question then, is money the only thing that is valued in our society? Many would argue that money makes the world go around and that one needs money in which to live in this world. I would agree with both of these sentiments. However, the amount of money one makes should not be the sole determinant of the value of one's degree. There are so many other important factors that provide value to one's education. In many ways the value of interdisciplinary and integrative learning is left to the student to define.

While some list interdisciplinary degrees as one of the worst paying college degrees the question is not really how much money a college graduate can make. Rather it should be centered on whether the college graduate is able to accomplish their life's goals and dreams, in part, through their learning and activities in college. Perhaps the interdisciplinary student's goal is to be a homemaker and stay-at-home parent. In college they learned about human development, psychology, music, and business. Their education could be viewed as highly valuable because they will be able to run an efficient home and be a better parent because they have an understanding of human development. They can help raise their children to be mentally healthy and maybe even learn to play an instrument. Perhaps another interdisciplinary student studies mechanical engineering, computer science, and business. Their degree might be highly valued because a company is on the verge of a significant breakthrough product and needs someone with those specific talents to help provide the missing piece. Perhaps earning a degree in itself is what is most valued to the individual learner. Western culture tends to place so much value on the extrinsic that they often forget that the intrinsic may be much more highly valued.

How will you value this interdisciplinary learning experience? How will you define this value to those who are interested? Your parents. Friends. Potential employers. The goal for you should be to construct an interdisciplinary learning experience that leads you toward one of your goals. Perhaps you want to work in a particular field that has no specific degree requirement. By the way, many careers options do not require college graduates to have a specific degree. As discussed earlier they do expect students to have particular sets of skills, almost none of these expectations are discipline specific. Even if you happened into an interdisciplinary learning experience, not as a choice but a degree completion strategy, you can still define value for your experience. Especially if you are in an interdisciplinary program that values integrative learning, you should be developing skills that employers will value.

As an interdisciplinary and integrative learner you will have critics for as long as you allow your learning to be criticized. Work to understand the advantages of interdisciplinary and integrative learning. Determine how your learning experiences apply to your career and future plans. Develop or construct your interdisciplinary story. It will be up to you to determine the value of your education and to let others know how you define it.

References

Benson, T. C. (1982). Five arguments against interdisciplinary studies. *Issues in Integrative Studies, 1*(1), 38–48.

Leonard, J. B. (2012). Integrative learning: A grounded theory. *Issues in Integrative Studies* (30), 48–74.

Newell, W. H. (1983). The case for interdisciplinary studies. *Issues in Integrative Studies, 2*, 1–19.

Newell, W. H. (2007). The role of interdisciplinary studies in the liberal arts. *LiberalArtsOnline, 7*(1).

CHAPTER 13

Job Hunting and Interdisciplinary Portfolios

In part, how you define the value of your interdisciplinary degree and experience will determine how you will proceed with the next step for your life. Let us assume, in the first part of this chapter, you are a typical age college student who will be looking to land their first career job after graduation. We will discuss some general information about best practices for job hunting, applying, interviewing, and etiquette. In the second part of this chapter we will discuss several different types of portfolios that will be helpful to you as you embark on the next part of your life's journey.

Job Hunting 101

The first question many of my students ask is, "where do you start?" There is no real secret here. Although we have many different tools available to us because of technology, the strategies are basically the same as they have always been. Look for jobs where people tend to post them. For people who are still associated with a university, utilize your college or university career center. Even the smallest colleges around the country have at least one person on campus that is knowledgeable in this area and can provide support. Utilize classified ads in newspapers and trade publications. If you are involved in organizations on your campus use the professional association as a way to network. **Networking** is the cultivating of relationships. If you are at a larger university with an active career center, get involved in their activities. If they host a career fair, attend. If they bring recruiters and employment agencies to campus, get on the notification list and cultivate relationships with these recruiters. Even if you are not ready to graduate, cultivating a relationship with a particular company is not difficult. Interview for an internship. Do a great job during your internship. Ask if you can do another internship the following semester but in a different area of the company. When you get ready to graduate, interview with the same company for an entry level career. You can also find jobs on company websites and utilizing the many job related websites and apps like Monster, Career Builder, and Glassdoor, for example.

There is no reason why a student could not easily locate 50 or more jobs they might be interested in. I recently had one student tell me he had 75 applications out.

Soon-to-be college graduates need to start preparing for the job market around the time they are a sophomore or junior. Starting this preparation may be vital to your ability to land a job after graduation. I tell my students that attending college away from home is, in part, about experiencing life in a different way. Some students tend to go overboard and experience too much of what life has to offer and forget about their studies, that other important part about attending college. In this age of social media, many college students post pictures of their conquests, spring break parties, post derogatory things about their school or professor, or in general make poor choices. The truth is once you post something to the Internet, it is there forever and it can have a serious impact on your future. CareerBuilder.com asked 2,500 hiring managers whether they look at social networking sites to find more information about prospective employees; 38% of managers said yes. Twenty-four percent of hiring managers said they found content that helped them make a decision to hire a candidate. Thirty-four percent of managers said they found content that warranted dismissal of a candidate. I sometimes tell the story I read about where an individual tweeted his excitement of landing the perfect job but complained about the hiring manager's tactics and long driving distance. The hiring manager read the tweet. When the candidate arrived home he had a message from the employer rescinding the job offer.

I digress; you have found several jobs you are interested in applying for, you have prepared and sent in your resume (which we will discuss in the next chapter), and now have an invitation to interview. Before you attend the interview, you will need to consider how your education, previous work experience, and other activities are related to the job you are seeking. You will also want to research the company for which you will be interviewing. One of the most common questions asked in an interview is "tell me what you know about us." You will want to be prepared with some information about the company in general and more specifically the job you are applying for. You can use the company website to do research. You may also want to call the company or do a site visit when possible. Prepare answers to other general interview questions and practice your answers. One good way to do this is to set up a mock interview with your school's career center. You do not want to sound rehearsed in the real interview, rather you want to sound confident.

When you show up for the interview you will want to take a good padfolio, which you can usually purchase at any office supply store. In the padfolio, you will want two or three copies of your resume with references. Although I talk more about this in the next chapter, recent college graduates typically do not have the experience to say to a potential employer, "you can have my reference upon request." You should have a list of five to ten insightful questions about the company. These questions should indicate your knowledge of and interest in the company. You should have a few letters of recommendation, a completed application, and possibly a copy of your transcript.

Double check the date, time, and place for your interview. There is nothing worse than showing up to the wrong place and at the wrong time. Some recruiters would look past this but in this tough job market it is better to be prepared than late. Usually arriving 15 minutes early is fine while 30 minutes is too early. I once had a friend that said if someone showed up 10 minutes early to a meeting, they were late. When you arrive make sure to treat the receptionist or person who greets you warmly. Do not mistake a low rank in position for low input. Including myself, there are many hiring managers that place a lot of value in the input of the front office person. They may have the power to positively or negatively pave your way before the interviewer meets you for the first time. It should go without saying, make sure you dress appropriately for your interview. For most interviews, business dress is appropriate, suit and tie for men, skirt or pant suit for women. There are few occasions where your dress might be atypical. For example, the retail store, Buckle, prefers job candidates to dress in their clothing for job interviews.

There is some etiquette involved in the interview process. Remember to be nice to the receptionist. When you do walk in to the interview room, be confident, introduce yourself, and shake hands with the interviewer. Do not sit until you are told where to sit. Make direct eye contact frequently with your interviewer and smile. During the interview, answer questions as succinctly as you can using examples of previous experience or learning when possible. Refrain from using filler words like "umm," "like," or "you know." Recruiters do not care about your past. They only ask about it in order to predict your future behavior. So do not be afraid to provide an example of a negative experience as long as you can discuss what you learned from it. When the interview is over ask for a business card. You will want to follow up the interview with a handwritten thank-you note. The thank-you note should thank the interviewer for their time, emphasize your interest in the position, and be personalized by including a memorable comment from the interview.

Types of Portfolios

Portfolios are portable collections or electronic spaces where you can showcase artifacts that communicate visually and verbally your identity, interest, skills, talents, and qualifications. There are several different types of portfolios you might consider developing. The type of portfolio you create is dependent to some extent on its function. There are job search or career planning portfolios, interview portfolios, graduate school portfolios, educational portfolios, and interdisciplinary portfolios. We will discuss a few of these in this section.

Career Planning Portfolios

Career Planning Portfolios are those constructed to help you manage your future plans. It will help keep you organized and prepared as you are searching for a job. You might use an electronic folder with subfolders or if you are the type of person that likes to feel the paper, a binder with tabs would work well. The career planning portfolio will include items like your master resume (which we will discuss in the next chapter), a generic cover letter, a generic and completed application, a collection of job openings you wish to apply for, a mechanism for keeping track of jobs you have applied for, interviewed with, which jobs you have been offered and not, and your response. You should also keep in this portfolio copies of recommendation letters, copies of licenses and certifications you may have, as well as a copy of your transcript. You might also have a section for your network list and any personal communication between you and hiring managers. You might also want to keep a copy of performance appraisals from previous jobs.

Interview Portfolios

Interview Portfolios are those that contain items that will be taken to an interview. In the previous section I discussed bringing a padfolio with a copy of your resume, references, application, and letters of recommendation. You might also include your own business card in this portfolio that you can give to the hiring manager or recruiter at the completion of your interview. The interview portfolio should also include a writing pad and pen for you to jot some important notes during the interview. Remember you are having a conversation with someone so you do not want to be staring at your notepad, use it if you need to.

Graduate School Portfolios

Graduate School Portfolios are those that are geared more towards applying to and being accepted into a graduate degree program. This portfolio might include some of the same information as the career planning portfolio but also include other types of information. For example, it might include a senior thesis or other significant papers you wrote in your undergraduate program. Some graduate programs may require a writing sample before acceptance.

Career Portfolios

Career Portfolios are those that include documented evidence or samples of your work related to the career you have or the career you want to enter. These documented samples are called **artifacts**.

Interdisciplinary Portfolios

Interdisciplinary portfolios could include aspects of all the portfolios mentioned previously. All portfolios should have a goal in mind. Interdisciplinary portfolios allow students to "claim ownership and authority over their writing, to review the papers they have written in college, to decide which ones they think are best, and to articulate their writing strengths" (Harrison, 1995, p. 45). The interdisciplinary portfolio is an opportunity to showcase your skills and abilities, those that are important to potential employers. The papers you have written, your engagement in certain learning activities, like service learning, study abroad, or undergraduate research, are all artifact opportunities. Interdisciplinary students who participate in service learning might include information about the project they worked on and its connection to learning or complex problem solving as an artifact. Interdisciplinary students should include relevant artifacts. Those that showcase a relevant skill, talent, or ability or those that highlight an application and value to interdisciplinary and integrative learning. Artifacts that are not typically relevant or useful to include are tests, quizzes, or samples where your grade was mediocre. Build a case that defines the value of your interdisciplinary learning experience. Be selective about the types of artifacts that you include in your portfolio. They should identify a specific skill or some area of knowledge that you have acquired. Ask yourself why do I need this particular artifact? What does it demonstrate? Will the reader have a sense of why I have included it? You might consider writing a brief paragraph before the actual artifact that would orient the reader to its importance. You may also consider writing a new piece after the artifact where you reflect on the assignment, what you learned, and how it identifies or demonstrates a specific skill, knowledge, or capability.

Constructing portfolios are not the most exciting part of the educational experience. At least I have rarely had a student say to me developing their portfolio was a fun experience. I have had students come back to me after graduation and say thank you for making me construct a portfolio. In fact, I had to create two different portfolios as part of my undergraduate and graduate experience. I hated doing both of them but never regretted the experience. Both of my portfolios were excellent tools for preparing me for life after graduation. My undergraduate portfolio was more of a career planning portfolio. I went back to it multiple times after graduation to collect important information as I was applying for jobs. In graduate school, I developed an education portfolio. It was one where I showcased my knowledge about education and classroom management. If I had pursued a career and primary or secondary education this would have been a very valuable tool for me.

The construction of your portfolio should actively engage you in the learning process. You should be able to reflect on particular artifacts and consider how far you have come, not just in knowledge accumulation but also in writing and communicating more effectively. I have often looked back at my previous work as an undergraduate and considered how my writing has increasingly improved. As you work on your portfolio, it should track your interdisciplinary and integrative learning skills. It should help you make connections between your curricular and co-curricular activities. It should help you build a bridge between your education and the real world.

Portfolios may also be utilized for making future career transitions. If you make portfolio development a practice for life rather than an assignment for school, you will have a product that will be useful for the rest of your life.

While you may think that choosing the right major is the key to getting a good job, your long-term professional success will depend far more on acquiring the right skills for the rapidly changing workplace and your ability to retool when needed. We have discussed these already but reconsider what employers are looking for in college graduates—the ability to work well in a team, a general understanding of science and technology and how these subjects are used in real world settings, the ability to write and speak well, the ability to think clearly about complex problems, the ability to analyze problems, and develop a workable solutions to those problem. Employers are looking for college graduates who are creative and innovative problem solvers and can apply knowledge and skills in new settings. Finally, employers want graduates with a strong sense of ethics and integrity. Ninety percent of employers say they are asking employees to take on more responsibilities and could use a broader set of skills. More than 80% of employers believe senior projects like a portfolio, internships, community based research, and research projects that help develop student's evidence based reasoning skills would help prepare them for success in today's workplace.

References

Harrison, S. (1995). Portfolios across the curriculum. *WPA: Writing Program Administration, 19*(2), 38–48.

CHAPTER 14

Interdisciplinary Resumes

In this chapter, we will discuss resumes, cover letters, and references. The information presented in this chapter comes from my experience as a hiring manager in several different fields and the years of experience I acquired working in career services at a university. I am of the opinion that resumes for interdisciplinarians are little different than those for disciplinarians. Therefore, we will discuss several different types of resumes and specific adjustments you might make to showcase your interdisciplinarity and other skills and experience. We will also discuss when additional information might make your resume stronger, how to avoid the most common resume mistakes, why a cover letter can increase your chances of getting hired, and who should or should not be on your reference list.

It has been my intention to help you see the advantages and value of interdisciplinary and integrative learning. Even if you may have ended up in an interdisciplinary program as part of a degree completion plan you should be able to discuss with others the value of your learning experience. James A. Baldwin said, "I've always believed that you can think positive just as well as you can think negative." I believe that. If you have thought of your interdisciplinarity or interdisciplinary degree program as a negative, it is time for you to reframe it in a more positive light. Your job search materials, cover letter, resume, and references should do just that.

Emphasize the Positive

In general, whether you are an interdisciplinarian or not, you need to consider how you will emphasize the positive aspects of your education, work experience, and related skills and abilities. The idea behind the primary job search documents is to present yourself to employers in such a way that will earn you more job interviews. While you may have had negative experiences during your education or at a job, the goal you need to keep in mind is to emphasize the positive. In the written materials, however, you do not want to discuss anything negative. Consider that a resume gets less than a minute (more like 15–30 seconds) of a potential employer's attention. I once had a recruiter tell me she had 1,500 resumes on her desk. For a frame of reference, that is three reams of paper. How much time do you think she could have given to each one of those resumes? Recruiters and hiring managers make decisions on who to bring in for interviews based primarily on the resume and sometimes the cover letter. The decision on whether you get the call to be interviewed could be based on something as simple as the type of paper or font you use.

Think of your resume as a one page advertisement or billboard. Whether you are a traditional or non-traditional student with more experience, one page is sufficient to get you to the next step. The only time I would recommend your resume be any longer is if you are applying to graduate school or a teaching job where they prefer a curriculum vitae (CV) rather than a resume. The resume should be focused and targeted toward a specific job requiring a certain set of skills and abilities. As you drive down the road a billboard has only a few seconds to make an impact on you, whether that is to give you information or invite you to try a product. Think of your resume like that. A hiring recruiter will make a decision about what you have to offer their company in the amount of time it takes you to review a billboard and make a decision about what is presented there. The importance of your resume cannot be overstated. It must be targeted to a specific job, it should emphasize the positive, it should be error free, and it should help you stand out among the crowd.

Types of Resumes

There are three standard resume formats that you might construct—the chronological resume, the functional/skills resume, and the combination resume. The **chronological resume** presents your experience, starting with the most recent position working backwards to the furthest work experience you have. The chronological resume is probably the most popular resume format and is most preferred by recruiters. This type of resume provides a very quick snapshot of your work history and the skills and abilities you have to offer the company. The **functional** or **skills resume** is one that is useful to students who have very little or no work experience. It is a good type of resume for college athletes because many of their skills and abilities come from being a part of an athletic team rather than traditional work experience. The challenge for students who have no work experience is how to develop a resume that highlights specific and related skills. The **combination resume** synthesizes the previous two types of resumes. Perhaps you have some work experience but nothing that is relevant to the job you are applying for. In this case you might list the jobs you have had but want to develop a resume that highlights specific and related skills and abilities.

Essential Information for the Resume

For every resume, there are four essential sections of information that should be included. The first section on every resume should be **contact information**. This section should probably be the largest section on your resume, in terms of font, and include your name, address, phone number, and email address. The next section should be **education**, where you list the degrees you have or will receive in order of most recent working backwards, the university from which they were conferred, and possibly your GPA. The bulk of your resume should be focused on the next section, **experience**, where you will discuss relevant work experience, skills, and abilities. The final section should contain any special **honors, certifications,** and **volunteer experience** you may have. I will discuss each one of these sections in more detail.

Your contact information should always be the very first section on your resume. It should include your name, where perhaps your name is in a slightly larger font than the rest of your resume. This section should include your mailing address. If you are considered a traditional student, I would encourage you to list two addresses, your current address and your permanent address (where your permanent address is your home where your parents live). This is important for traditional students because sometimes employers may look at your resume, even interview you, but for some reason decide to offer the position to someone else. However, they keep your resume on file for future reference. In my experience as a career counselor, I have had this very thing happen; where after a student graduated the employer called back looking for that student. Because that student only put their current university address on their resume, it was impossible to find them. Make sure you also have current phone number(s) on your resume. I would encourage you to have your cell phone number and a permanent phone number where you can be contacted or a message can be left for you. Make sure a professional email address is listed on your resume. I will discuss some etiquette as it relates to your email address and cell phone in just a moment. First consider some other tips for completing your contact information. Do not abbreviate—write out "street," "road," "avenue," and so forth. Make it very clear how to get in touch with you. Use the current postal abbreviations for States (e.g., NY, NJ, CA for California) and include your zip code. Make sure someone will be able to mail you a letter using the listed contact information. Write out your phone number without parentheses. Use a dash or period in between the numbers.

In the previous chapter I briefly discussed the need for students to start making a transition from college student to professional around their sophomore or junior year. While that discussion was centered primarily on your online social presence, there are some other areas of etiquette you need to consider. Both your cell phone voicemail and email address should project a professional image, one that says "I am an adult and ready for the workplace." If your cell phone voicemails says something like, "Hey it's the weekend, time to party, leave me a message" or "I'm busy getting drunk, leave me a message, and I'll call you when I sober up," that may be humorous to you and your friends, but a potential employer will not find it very funny and take that kind of behavior to mean you are not yet ready for a career. The same is true for your email address. It does not portray a professional image to have an email address such as "sexymom@gmail.com" or "playboy69@yahoo.com". You want to have an email address that is very professional. One that may be similar to your university assigned email address. A very professional email address could be as simple as "firstname.lastname@server.com". You do not have to spend money to have a professional email address. Create one that helps you project a professional image as you search for that perfect job.

Your education section should be the very next section after contact information. Because you will be a recent graduate or someone who is about to graduate, you want this information to be prominent but simple. Here is an example:

Best University, Anytown TX
Bachelor of Science in Degree Name
GPA 3.7
Graduation: May 201X

If you are earning an interdisciplinary degree, you might consider listing your areas of concentration or those that are most relevant. For example:

Best University, Anytown TX
Bachelor of Science in Interdisciplinary Studies
Areas of Concentration: Petroleum Engineering, Organizational Leadership, & Human Resource Development
GPA 3.7
Graduation: May 201X

Notice that I did not abbreviate any information in this example. If you were to put PE, for example, recruiters may not know that it is short for Petroleum Engineering. You may want to list your grade point average (GPA) on your resume. The caveat is that your GPA should be above a 3.0. There should be no references to high school on your resume. Do not list your high school graduation, honors, or organizations that you were a part of. What you did in high school has almost no relevance now that you have earned a college degree.

The next section, and the most important, is where you will discuss your work experience. Or if you are developing a functional/skills resume, you will develop this section in terms of relevant skills and abilities. This section includes any full-time and part-time paid employment. If you completed an internship or practicum as part of your education (I would highly encourage you to), you would list that work experience here. Volunteer work will most likely be included in the optional fourth section. However, anything that would be considered work experience—self-employment, work in a family business, and military service—should be placed in this section.

In this section, start by listing your position and the name of the company you worked for and dates of employment. Then provide the location, by city and state. The full address is not needed here. For example:

Employee   Great Place to Work, Anytown TX   May, 2010–Present

---

Remember space is at a premium for your one page advertisement. You should look for ways to lessen the verbiage on your resume without abbreviating terms people may be unfamiliar with. After you have listed your position and place of employment, describe your most relevant responsibilities and accomplishments. Often, students will write something like "cashier" as a description of their duties. While this is descriptive of your job function and most people can envision what you did, it does not provide enough relevant detail of skills and abilities you may have. It is important to discuss the responsibilities you had as part of your job function. For example, you might discuss the amount of money or number of sales you were responsible for per day, week, or month. Consider other relevant skills and abilities related to the job you want and the job you are discussing. Is proficiency in 10 key typing required? A cash register is set up to use 10 key so you might discuss this.

As you discuss the relevant skills and abilities of your work experience it is good practice to have between three to five bulleted points describing those skills and abilities or in some cases writing a brief narrative in paragraph form. If you are using bulleted points begin each description with an action verb. For example, "Generated 10,000 sales totaling more than $50,000 per month." If you worked as server in a restaurant, writing something like "Took reservations and takeout orders by phone" or "served food and beverages efficiently" are not particularly good examples. Those two examples describe more of a function rather than a skill or ability. Also, when you are writing out these descriptions use the correct tense. If you currently work as a server, you would not use the past tense to describe your skills. Some recruiters like to see numbers or some type of quantitative evaluation of your skills and abilities. Make sure each point is clearly relevant in some way to the job you are applying for. Try to describe portable or transferable skills you may possess.

After you have discussed your relevant work experience you might also want to list other relevant experiences, skills, or abilities. You may want to briefly list any additional languages you speak, certifications, or licenses you hold. Again the idea is to be relevant with any information you decide to include on your resume. This final section is also the place where you can discuss more about who you are by listing honors, awards, or activities. If you were the president of a particular sorority or fraternity this would be listed at the bottom of your resume in this section. Prestigious scholarships you may have been awarded would go in this section. Being selected for the President's list or Dean's list would be appropriate for this section.

Master Resume

Whether you are an interdisciplinarian or not, it would be useful to create a **master resume,** which is a document that includes descriptions of everything you have ever done related to education, work, and service. It is more like a CV than a resume. This document is important to keep updated because, as we mentioned earlier, your resume should be one page in length. It is impossible to include everything and the goals of your resume are to emphasize the positive and produce something relevant to the position you are applying for. In the work experience section, you must be selective. Having a master resume allows you to customize a resume by copying information from the master that is related to a very specific job description. You will find that every job you apply for has a specific job description that discusses the expectations, requirements, and qualifications for the right candidate. Your resume should be crafted in such a way that reads as if you are the right candidate. You should never use the same resume to apply for different jobs; always tailor it. Once your master resume is complete, send it to multiple people for feedback.

There are some common mistakes or errors that students often make on resumes. Avoid including irrelevant personal information, your marital status, age, gender, or a picture (unless required). However, most of this information is irrelevant and could lead to discriminatory hiring practices. Ensure your resume is free of grammatical and spelling errors. Never lie on your resume. There are several words that people often use incorrectly; there, their, and they're; affect and effect, make sure you use words in their proper context. Make sure your position as an "Assistant Manager" does not read as an "Ass. Manger". After you have your resume completed and it is ready, send it to your friends and family for review. Double and triple check it for errors before you send it to the recruiter.

Online Resumes & Applications

Online resumes are becoming increasingly important. One great tool for creating an online resume is Linkedin. While I think creating this type of online professional presence is important it is also necessary to understand the different procedures in applying for a job online as opposed to physically handing in a resume or job application. Many companies have moved almost entirely to an electronic process for collecting application materials from candidates. The process may be handled through email or through an online application system. One primary item of importance is to ensure you follow the formatting instructions exactly and include the items requested of you before you hit "send" or "submit." Some companies use a sophisticated computer algorithm to automatically reduce the number of applicants to those most qualified. So the first run of applicants is handled by a computer not a human being. If you fail to follow instructions exactly the computer may not recognize your application as complete and you will not be considered for the position. Another important aspect of applying for jobs online, especially when a computer is the first to review your application, is to use as many applicable keywords as possible from the job description. Again, a master resume would be very helpful here, you can tailor your application and resume based on the job description.

Cover Letters

The cover letter introduces your resume when you will be emailing or mailing it to a hiring manager. It increases your chance of being invited for an interview in part because you have an opportunity to be more persuasive in your discussion of how you are qualified for the position. The resume is pretty standard; generally everyone's resume will look similar in nature. So the cover letter may allow you to stand out from the crowd and highlight relevant skills and abilities that you possess. As in the resume, you should utilize relevant key words from the job description in the cover letter. The cover letter is also a key part of your advertisement, so remember to emphasize the positive.

There are many opinions on how to write a good cover letter. There are almost 44 million results on a google search for "writing a good cover letter." Here is my opinion. The cover letter should include three brief paragraphs and address the position you are applying for, relevant skills and abilities, and a professional closing.

In the first paragraph, you should clearly state the position you are applying for, using the exact wording from the job posting and where you found the job posting. For example, "My name is John Smith and I am writing to apply for the Assistant Manager of Sales position found on Careerbuilder.com." In this first paragraph you might also list some specific qualification for the position. Perhaps the posting requires you to have a college degree; you could say, "I am a recent graduate of the Best University where my education was focused on sales."

The second paragraph is used to highlight your relevant skills and abilities that match the job description. Again, just like the resume, the cover letter should be tailored. You do not want to submit the same cover letter for every job you apply to. As the hiring manager for my department, one thing that really frustrates me is when I receive applications to teach in my program and the cover letter is generic, addressed to someone else, or does not address my academic program. For example, I sometimes get cover letters that discuss how much education and experience the applicant has in the field of nursing. Because my academic program has nothing to do with nursing, I immediately know this person has made a costly error or is lazy. I immediately assign these applications as not qualified. When I get a cover letter that is addressed to some other director or where the content of the letter is written towards another job, I assume they are not interested in applying for my job posting or my job opening is not important enough for the applicant to take great care in applying. This is not the type of person I want working in my department. As you craft your resume and cover letter take care to write it towards the specific job you are applying for, go the extra mile to find out who the hiring manager is, I believe it will make a difference. Finally, in the third paragraph you should thank the reviewer, ask for the interview, and indicate in a professional manner what this particular job/company means to you. It probably goes without saying, but the cover letter must be free from grammatical or spelling errors.

Let us assume for a moment that you will be sending in your resume and cover letter as an email attachment to a recruiter. In the subject line of your email, you should be very specific about the reason for your writing; for example, "Job Application for Assistant Manager of Sales." In the body of your email, your salutation should be formal and professional. In fact, in all of your communication you should be somewhat formal, even more so with people you do not know. For example, you should write a professional salutation: "Dear Mr. Johnson." Provide a specific label for any file attachments that you will submit as part of your resume or cover letter. For example, you may want to name your resume file using a protocol similar to 'firstinitiallastname_resume' and one that is similar for your cover letter. With the rise in hacking attempts of business and the ease at which viruses can be downloaded onto the computer, generic files sent from an unknown person rarely get opened by me. If I receive an email with an attached labeled "document one", I will likely delete it without reading the email or opening the file. A potential employer who may not know you will likely do the same. When using email and online systems to apply for jobs, be very clear about the attachments. Use the body of the email to write a three sentence version of your cover letter. As you end your email, be very professional, include a signature line with your full name and contact information. Avoid text abbreviations, emoticons, and any kind of fancy backgrounds or unusual fonts.

References and Recommendations

It has been my practice over the years to require my students to include references with their resume. As mentioned earlier, most soon to be or recent college graduates do not have the experience necessary to list "References Available by Request" on their resume. To be able to submit a one page resume students need to be able to print their references on the back of that same page. Generally speaking students should list four to six references on their resume. The best references are those people who will speak positively about your performance. Before listing someone as a reference on your resume, you should speak with that person to seek their permission and discuss the ways in which they might positively portray who you are as a person.

I learned this lesson the hard way. I once worked for a person for a couple of years. We had a fairly good relationship and when I left, it was amicable. Although I was not happy I gave the requisite notice and did not bad mouth the employer or company. I made several assumptions that were incorrect, first that because I left on friendly terms he would provide a good reference and second he would honor what he said. Fast forward a couple of years, I randomly saw him at a local store. He mentioned that he would be happy to serve as a reference or do what he could to help if I ever needed it. I took him at his word and listed him as a reference when I applied to another position. I ended up getting the job but during my first week or two, my new boss came to me and said "you know this reference you have on your resume? You should probably think about taking them off your reference list. He gave you a horrible recommendation." I was really shocked. My boss told me they thought nothing of it because all my other references were glowing. To think that someone could or would do that is unconscionable.

The moral of that story is to make sure you know, to the extent possible, what others will say about you. You want those who will speak to your related skills, abilities, and emphasize the positive. The best references are easy to reach and will follow up promptly with requests. When you apply for a job and get a request for an interview, follow up with your reference list to let them know they may be receiving a call. Provide full contact information for your reference including, their name, title, mailing address, phone number, and email address. Carry your typed reference list to all interviews and include it on the back of your resume.

CHAPTER 15

Graduation and Graduate School

As we come to the end of this textbook, I think about an old saying attributed to Harvey MacKay, "find something you love to do and you will never have to work a day in your life." As a student who is preparing to graduate, either you are considering your next steps or someone (a parent perhaps) is hounding you about what you will do when you graduate. As an interdisciplinarian, the answer to this question is sometimes very difficult. Because we have a penchant towards learning, focusing in on a particular type of work we will do is challenging. What I encourage students to do is to narrow the scope of their focus to only the next three to five years. Consider something you would love to do for the next few years, and make that your career or learning goal. Is it concentrating on doing research or obtaining a higher level of education? Perhaps graduate school is the next step for you. Would you prefer to utilize the skills and abilities you have acquired over the last few years of your undergraduate program in a career? Perhaps launching into an entrepreneurial adventure is for you. Whatever you choose, consider something that motivates you to get up in the morning.

Graduation and the Job Search

In the previous chapter, we discussed some job search strategies and tools you would need during your search for a new career. In this section I want to discuss a few items that may be helpful to you as you make a decision about what to do next in your life. Sometimes it can be helpful to think about big decisions in manageable chunks of information or steps. Assume that after graduation your next step is landing that first career job rather than graduate school. Next you will need to make a decision concerning the right career for you. Earning an interdisciplinary degree may open multiple career options in different fields. The areas of learning you chose to concentrate in may strengthen your qualifications and highlight specific skills necessary to do a number of different things. To make the right decision about a career will involve a process of self-discovery that will help you identify some of your key interests and skills and how they might relate to different career options. I recommend students take multiple career assessments like StrengthsQuest®, FOCUS, Strong Interest Inventory, or TypeFocus. Any of these assessments will tell you a lot about yourself. Taking multiple assessments will provide to you a more complete picture. If you have taken any kind of assessment similar to the ones mentioned above but it has been a while, I would encourage you to go back and review that information or perhaps take the assessment again. Our personalities, our skills, and abilities do change over time. In this step of making a decision, it is also important to talk to people about what they see are your strengths and weaknesses. Visit with your parents, coworkers, fellow students, professors, or schedule a visit with a career counselor at your university. Once you know more about yourself and have made a decision about the career field you want to go into, it may be helpful to develop your career objective.

Secondly, while developing a **career objective** or **personal profile statement** is important, let me be clear that I do not believe college students should have this on their resume unless it is something that is expected in the career field they are applying to. Again, there are many opinions about whether to have the career objective be a part of the resume, this happens to be mine. This task is more about developing a career objective that you can use to guide your journey. It may become your **elevator speech** which is a short pitch of who you are and what skills and abilities you can bring to a company. Typically you will need to be able to describe and sell yourself in 30 seconds or less. Your career objective can be used as an introductory statement in a cover letter. Whether it is career objective, personal profile statement, or elevator speech it should relate to a targeted career, targeted employer, introduce key skills, and express an interest in a specific position. You might construct your career objective using a brief one-line description of skills related to a specific position and how you would utilize those skills if you were given an opportunity to work in that particular company. For example: "I'm seeking a position as a family and consumer science teacher in a large high school with an emphasis on child development. I'm submitting my application for job posting number found on the ISD website." This career objective is clear and concise. A personal profile might include a bit more information and be most relevant for people with extensive work experience. For example, "I'm a highly qualified and detail oriented design professional with demonstrated leadership and success in the areas of interior and exterior design and project management. I have excellent analytical communication, computer, and organizations skills, am bilingual: English and Spanish, and I'm submitting my application for the [specific job announcement] found on the firm's HR website." Notice again, how specific, clear, and concise the statement is. Work to provide well written, well-crafted personal profile statements that centers itself on categories of skills and abilities rather than a specific objective. Now that you have more information about yourself and have developed a career objective or personal profile statement you should engage in research about specific companies you might want to work for.

The third step is to conduct industry research. As you search for jobs you will find many that will be of interest to you. I advise students to spend time doing research on a specific industry or a specific company rather than casting a wide and general net. Researching specific industries, companies, and jobs will give you greater insight for crafting your targeted resume and targeted cover letter. Utilize job sites like Monster, CareerBuilder, Glassdoor, and Indeed to find job openings in specific areas of the country or world within a specific industry of interest. Once you find several job openings you want to apply for, start preparing yourself and the information you will need to submit; the resume, cover letter, references, etc. If you developed a master resume and job search portfolio you will already have access to much of the information you need. Although the economy has improved, finding a job can still be difficult. You may spend significant amounts of time looking for a job. When you are having trouble, consider other sources of job leads; friends of family and family of friends.

If your job search has included walking into places you might like to work and asking to fill out a resume, make sure you go in prepared for the interview. Everything counts when looking for a job. Treat every opportunity you have as an interview or as a potential interview. Come dressed appropriately and have copies of your resume available. Display confidence about yourself and your ability to do a job. Bring your interview portfolio with you. Your interview portfolio should have copies of your resume, copies of your business card, your reference list, and a completed generic application.

The fourth step has been stated before, make sure you engage in as much networking as possible. I advise my students to utilize a professional online networking tool like Linkedin. When you are looking for a job, include coworkers, supervisors, instructors, family and friends, anybody you can think of who might be able to help you find that first job after graduation. One idea that I sometimes recommend to students when they want to work in a company and have no experience in that particular industry is to do an **informational interview**. An informational interview is when you meet with a potential business professional to learn about their company or industry before applying for a job in that company or industry. This can be a valuable experience even if you do not apply for a job with that specific company. You will have met someone you might be able to add to your network. You will have more information about a specific company and industry than you did prior to the interview. You may have also worked your way into a potential job interview by engaging in this activity. You have probably heard the phrase "it is not what you know but who you know." The informational interview gives you an opportunity to meet someone new and open new potential opportunities for you. If you do utilize this strategy make sure to take a business card. Thank them for the interview and the opportunity they provided to learn more about their business. Once you find a job or first career do not throw your job search portfolio away; keep it and continue revising it. You may find yourself in two or three years needing another job or ready to change careers. Maybe a job is not where you will be headed after graduation. Perhaps the next step for you is graduate school. In this next section I want to share with you some tips and advice I wish I had known before going to graduate school.

Preparing for Graduate School

I am a first generation college graduate. As a result I did not have anyone in my family to lean on, to ask questions about college and certainly not graduate school. Graduate school is not for everyone. You should not make an arbitrary decision to go to graduate school, it should be a very thoughtful process. Much like the job search tips I shared above, making a decision to go to graduate school may begin with a period of self-discovery.

I earned my undergraduate and master's degrees through distance and online programs. They were both a good fit for me professionally because I was working fulltime and had a young family. Beginning my master's degree was not too difficult as I knew what I wanted to study. What I was not prepared for was the higher expectation in terms of my written communication. The quantity and quality of written assignments I was expected to complete was much higher than when I was an undergraduate student. I was also not prepared for the final steps to completing my first graduate degree. Granted, my lack of understanding or preparedness is likely due to being in an online program rather than an on campus program, but I was not aware until a week prior that I was expected to complete what is known as a comprehensive exam. At that time I was not aware of what a comprehensive exam was. A **comprehensive exam** is one you typically take at the end of your graduate degree experience. It is usually an essay exam where you are expected to recall information from the courses you took over the last two to four years in order to answer the questions you will be presented with. I have never known a comprehensive exam to allow materials inside the testing area. The exam must be completed using only what you can recall by memory and most exams expect you to be able to properly cite and reference information. It was a good thing I paid attention and read my material; otherwise, I might not be sitting here typing out this chapter. When I decided to go on to earn a doctorate I would have an entirely new academic experience. I knew very little about doctoral programs and expectations for completion. I made some attempts to contact others but most had no real experience. So I had little idea of what to expect in a doctoral program. I did not realize the kind of commitment I was making to earn a terminal degree. I was also not prepared for how different the on campus environment was to the online learning environment.

Below are five considerations as you work to decide whether graduate school is for you.

1. Why are you going to graduate school instead of getting a job?
2. Why is it important to you?
3. When should you consider a graduate degree?
4. What's the best graduate school or program for you?
5. Can you afford graduate school?

First, why are you considering graduate school? Are you considering it because there is a job that you want and they require a master's or doctoral degree? If so, that might be a good reason to consider going to graduate school. However, if you are considering this as an option because it seems like the next logical step, you may want to reconsider. Not all careers require an advanced degree. Consider whether an advanced degree will add value to your career in terms of portability, promotability, and finances. Earning a graduate degree is an incredible time commitment, as well as a financial and relational commitment. If you are married or committed to a significant other, you should be prepared to spend less time on that relationship to accommodate for your academic experience. There should be a clear goal or reason for considering graduate school. It may be important for you to stay marketable in your field. Perhaps earning a graduate degree will help you retool for a career change. In part, I chose to pursue an advanced degree as a way to retool. I earned an undergraduate degree in church ministries, which was great because full-time ministry was my career at the time. After 15 years, I was ready to do something different but perhaps related. I knew an advanced degree was the best choice for me because it did not make sense to earn a second undergraduate degree. Teaching has always been a passion of mine and I tried to consider the next 10 to 15 years of my life. A graduate degree in education seemed to make the most sense. Again, I wanted to retool for some future plans so after finishing my graduate degree I enrolled in a doctoral program where I could do research that would support a non-profit organization my wife and I founded.

Graduate school should not be considered the default move or used as an excuse to avoid getting a job. If that is the case, you will probably find yourself getting frustrated with the increased demands and the time commitment. The reasons for going straight to graduate school after earning an undergraduate degree might be you are accustomed to being a student and have a strong momentum for your advanced education. Perhaps your study skills are sharp or you have few occupational or relational obligations. You may want to consider working for a few years before going to graduate school. Doing so will provide you a different perspective of the experience. I think of graduate school as requiring a professional perspective. I look at is as more of a job. Yes you go to class, yes you have to do assignments, lots of assignments, but the experience is different. You work more closely with your professors especially in a doctoral program. It is more like being a colleague rather than a student. If you are considering a terminal degree so that you might be a professor one day, I would also encourage you to gain some valuable work experience outside of the university. I had professors that were well noted experts in their field and theoretically knew what they were talking about, but they had no applicable experience outside of the university. Some of my favorite professors were those that could discuss their research in terms of its real life applicability because they had experience from outside the walls of an institution.

How do you choose the best graduate school? In part, this question is best answered by your thoughts about why you want to go to graduate school in the first place. Some things to consider are the recognition of the university, college, department, and faculty. Is the university accredited? What is the reputation of the university? Will you be proud to tell someone you earned a degree from a particular institution? Does the institution have a good reputation for working with students and offering opportunities to research, publish, and earn money? Does the institution offer what you want to study? Will the institution help you get a job afterwards? Is there a particular professor that you want to study with? Maybe you are really interested in research and you want to work with a particular professor. Will they even accept you? You should ask yourself about the quality of life. Can you afford to go to graduate school? What does it cost public vs. private? How long is it going to take you? What kind of commitment are you going to need to make in order to go through this graduate program? If you are working, does your company offer tuition reimbursement? There is so much to consider when deciding whether graduate school is for you. Even when you think you have answered all of these questions and have chosen a great school you still take a bit of a chance. Consider the news report about a wealthy historic college closing, watch a news story about it here http://www.cbsnews.com/news/closing-of-sweet-briar-college-signals-turmoil-for-higher-education/

Let us assume that you have made the decision. You are going to graduate school. Congratulations! Now you need to take the appropriate steps to get into your desired institution and program. You will need to take the **GRE,** which is a standardized exam similar to the SAT or ACT, but is required for you to enter most accredited graduate school programs. Some programs require a particular score and others simply require that you have taken it. You will want to check with your institution for their requirements. There is a deadline for submitting applications for graduate school and many institutions have a two-step application process where you will submit a general application to the graduate school and another to the college or department where your degree originates from. As part of your application you will likely need to prepare a resume and writing samples. Some schools require that you submit a cover letter, letters of references, and write an essay. Some graduate programs will require you to go through an interview before being accepted. Physical Therapy Schools, Occupational Therapy Schools, Marriage and Family Therapy programs, sometimes Counselor Education or Psychology programs will require you to do individual interviews, group or panel interviews, and mock counseling sessions. Prepare for that interview just as you would a job interview.

Consider that class offerings are generally different at the graduate level. Most classes meet once or twice a week for three hours at a time. You will be expected to discuss material in class rather than listening to your professor lecture. In some advanced graduate courses you may be expected to teach the class or part of the class during the semester. Exams in graduate school are typically essays papers, essay exams, rarely are they the multiple choice/true-false type exam as in most undergraduate courses. You are expected to think at a much higher level, to critically think about the material, to synthesize it in such a way that you can make sense of it in written form. The level of thought expected of you in graduate school is exponentially higher than in your undergraduate program.

Many graduate programs provide a fellowship or assistantship to help supplement tuition costs. Typically an assistantship includes a monthly financial stipend, so you get a paycheck every month, but it may also include some discounts on tuition and/or fees. The advice I have for you here is request it early and if the program director does not mention it, you need to ask about it.

Going to graduate school is a very different experience than your undergraduate experience. It can be a great and very rewarding experience. I have found it to be so. Just like in most jobs you will have over your lifetime, you will get out of graduate school what you put into it. If you treat it like any undergraduate academic experience you may not enjoy yourself and you may not be allowed to stay in the program. As I mentioned above, I found graduate school to be much more professional than the undergraduate experience. If you do not operate in such a way, you may find yourself being "fired" from the graduate program.

Whatever your next step in life is, make a plan to be successful. You have probably heard the saying "those that fail to plan, plan to fail." Set goals for yourself whether in the area of learning or what you want to achieve in your career. Having a goal gives you something to work towards, something to achieve. The former chancellor at my current university used to say, "dream no little dreams" and the university motto was "from here it's possible." As we come to the end of this textbook I would echo those statements and encourage you to plan for a great future.

CPSIA information can be obtained at www.ICGtesting.com
Printed in the USA
LVOW03s2359080515

437800LV00001B/1/P